Klaus Wolfsperger
Annette Miehle-Wolfsperger

La Gomera

Translated by Tom Krupp

44 selected walks on the coasts
and in the mountains of the wildest of the Canary Islands

With 96 colour photographs, 44 walking maps with a scale of 1:50,000
as well as an overview map with a scale of 1:150,000

ROTHER · MUNICH

Cover photo:
Terraces in the upper Valle Gran Rey.

Frontispiece (photo on page 2):
On the trail from El Guru into Barranco de Arure.

All photographs are by the authors.

Cartography:
Walking maps with a scale of 1:50,000 © Freytag & Berndt, Vienna, overview maps with scales of 1:150,000 / 1:300,000 © Klaus Wolfsperger

Translation:
Tom Krupp

1st edition 2003
© Bergverlag Rother GmbH, Munich

ISBN 3-7633-4823-9

Distributed in Great Britain by Cordee, 3a De Montfort Street, Leicester
Great Britain LE1 7HD, www.cordee.co.uk

ROTHER WALKING GUIDES

Andalusia South · Azores · Corsica · Côte d'Azur · Crete East · Crete West · Cyprus · Gomera · Gran Canaria ·
Iceland · La Palma · Madeira · Mallorca · Mont Blanc · Norway South · Provence · Pyrenees 1 · Sardinia · Sicily
· High Tatra · Tenerife · Tuscany North · Valais East · Valais West · Around the Zugspitze

**Dear mountain lovers! We would be happy to hear your opinion
and suggestions for amendment to this Rother walking guide.**

BERGVERLAG ROTHER · Munich
D-85521 Ottobrunn · Haidgraben 3 · Tel. (089) 608669-0, Fax -69
Internet www.rother.de · **E-mail** bergverlag@rother.de

Preface

La Gomera, the second smallest Canary Island, is surely the most untamed isle of the Canary archipelago. From the central highlands, reaching to about 1500 m above sea level, not less than 50 deep-cut gorges slice the island like a cake on their erosive journey to the sea; otherwise Gomera, barely 25 km in diameter, is fairly gentle-sloped. While in many regions the valleys boast picturesque palm groves, cultivated terraces and small hamlets, the mountainous areas are dominated by deep laurel woods.

La Gomera is a walking paradise par excellence. Anyone searching for an adventure far away from the raucous tourist traps will find this holiday spot a very good tip. Despite the recent wave of tourism, the island still remains one of the most pristine and difficult to penetrate of the Canary Islands. Opinions differ as to the best choice of holiday resorts. San Sebastián offers the best bus connections. While the southern island around Santiago boasts the most sunshine, the north, although often cloud-covered due to the trade winds, charms with its ever-verdant valleys. Of course, Valle Gran Rey is the favourite choice for most holiday-makers, offering enchanting seaside resorts and, at the same time, fascinating and diverse scenery.

This walking guide presents you with a wide range of captivating routes which include all the island's regions. The selection spans from pleasant paths through idyllic palm-covered valleys to tranquil high mountain rambles leading to panoramic peaks – walking trails through misty magical tropical forests were taken into consideration as well as the *caminos*, sometimes stone-paved, that were the main connecting routes for villages in times gone by. Also attractive are the sheer steep coastlines, solitary beaches, dramatic gorges and bright, verdant pine forests. Many of the suggested routes are extremely well-suited for the less-experienced walker. Veteran mountain hikers not timorous in the face of Herculean undertakings and who thrive on a shot of adventure as well as a bit of a thrill, will find a wealth of routes to choose from.

The present edition has been thoroughly updated, however, constant changes caused by the forces of Nature and by the intervention of human beings, may alter the routes in many different ways. Therefore, we would appreciate any corrections or alterations sent to the publisher. At the same time, we would like to express our heartfelt thanks for the many friendly letters received from our readers in regards to our guides.

We wish you many lovely and adventurous days during your holidays on Gomera.

Fall 2003   Klaus and Annette Wolfsperger

Contents

Tourist Information

Use of the guide

The most important information for each of the suggested walks is summarised as a list of key points. After a short description of the main characteristics of the walk, a detailed route description is given. The coloured walking map is marked with a line following the route. All walking destinations, place names, starting and finishing points and all important points en route are listed in the index at the back of the book. The overview map on the back cover pinpoints the locations of the individual walks.

Grade

Most of the walks follow distinct paths and trails, however, this should not detract from the fact that some walks demand a strong physical condition, sure-footedness, a head for heights and orientation skills. Walkers should also take into consideration that the difficulties might significantly increase during periods of bad weather. To help you judge the difficulty of the suggested walks more easily, the route numbers are colour-coded as follows:

Cairns on the route to the Cuevas Blancas; in the background – Tenerife's Teide.

Alto del Contadero – Hermigua

The cavalcade tour of the island – descent through the laurel forest (Walk 43; 3¾ hrs, possible ascent to Garajonay).

Degollada de Peraza – Roque de Agando – Playa de Santiago

Via Walk 3 to Roque de Agando, descent to Santiago with Walk 6 (5¾ hrs).

Agulo – Juego de Bolas

Circuit walk with spectacular stretches and plenty of variety (Walk 37; 4 hrs).

Chipude – Fortaleza – Garajonay

Pleasant high ramble with Fortaleza excursion (Walks 14 and 13; 5 hrs).

Arure – Taguluche

Majestic extendable circuit route (Walk 31; 4½ hrs).

Vallehermoso – El Tión

Scenically impressive circuit walk to Roque El Cano (Walk 36; 3½ hrs).

Valle Gran Rey – El Cercado

Extensive circuit route with exquisite views (Walk 23; 6 hrs).

Barranco de Guarimiar

Spectacular gorge walk (Walk 9; 3¾ hrs).

Degollada de Peraza – El Cabrito

Fascinating circuit route through the idyllic and untamed south (Walk 5; 7 hrs).

Barranco de Argaga

Adventurous ascent through a craggy labyrinth (Walk 27; 5½ hrs).

El Cercado – Las Hayas – Arure – La Mérica – Valle Gran Rey

Pleasant panoramic walk (Walk 30; 3¾ hrs, possible excursion to Jardín de la Creces, Walk 18).

Valle Gran Rey – Vallehermoso

Incredible crossing through the laurisilva forest (Walk 22; 5¼ hrs).

BLUE

These walks follow paths which are generally wide and only moderately steep – thus relatively harmless, even in poor weather. They can also be undertaken in the company of children and older walkers without great danger.

RED

These footpaths and climbs are often narrow, and short stretches can be somewhat precipitous. For these reasons, these walks should only be undertaken by the sure-footed, experienced hiker. Some stretches could demand a fair sense of orientation.

BLACK

These climbs are mostly narrow and very steep. Some stretches can be dangerously exposed and/or slope crossings can be dangerously slippery underfoot. Sometimes scrambling skills, even requiring handholds, may be necessary. This means that these routes should only be attempted by the sure-footed, physically fit and experienced mountain hiker who has a good head for heights and well-developed orientation skills.

Approach
Most of the walks can be reached by public busses. These are often full, in addition, the connections are few and far between and the usual service is targeted to the schedules of the ferries in San Sebastián and the airport near Santiago. Service between Santiago, Valle Gran Rey, Vallehermoso and Hermigua are virtually non-existent, while other regions are completely cut off. For these reasons, many routes must be approached by car or taxi. More specific information regarding the approach is included in the walk description.

Walking times
The times indicated represent only the actual walking time – not including rest stops or snapshot breaks. Usually the times for the individual stages and total times will be cited.

Equipment
Sturdy shoes with non-slip soles, durable trousers, sunscreen and possibly a hat, protective gear for wind, rain and cold as well as hiking provisions for the walk (sufficient liquids!) are required for most routes.

Dangers
Most walks lead along well-maintained, distinct trails. Extremely precipitous or demanding stretches will be indicated in the route description. Along the mountain slopes and over the ridges always expect fog, brought in by the trade winds, which can present the walker with serious orientation problems. On the ridgelines, strong and gusty winds may well develop, similar to the »Föhn« storms occurring in the Alps. After periods of rainfall, avoid *barrancos* and steep, exposed mountain slopes.

Best times of the year
Gomera can be walked year-round. In the winter months (November – April), the weather is not quite as predictable as in summer: heavy showers are not at all rare. During the warm, sometimes quite hot, months of summer, better avoid walks along or near the coast.

Refreshment and Accommodation
Mountain huts providing food and drink, like those found in the Alps, are non-existent. Instead, along the way, refreshment can be enjoyed from time to time in bars and restaurants. Many routes pass abandoned, mostly dilapidated houses or pass caves that can be used as shelter during inclement weather.

Nature and the environment
Please respect the flora and fauna – bring your refuse back with you for proper disposal (what you pack in, pack out!) – do not carelessly throw cigarette stubs away and do not make open fires (danger of forest fire!).

Herd of goats at the edge of the trail.

Maps

We recommend the Freytag&Berndt map with a scale of 1:35,000, the Goldstadt map with a scale of 1:50,000 and the topographical Mapa Guía with a scale of 1:50,000. The 5-part series of maps with a scale of 1:25,000 from the Instituto Geográfico Nacional are wonderfully detailed – however, many of the trails are not depicted in these topographical maps.

Tips for linear and long-distance hikers

Some routes suggested are conceived as linear walks, with destinations far away from the starting points. For these, we recommend to either use public transportation (bus, taxi), join an organised walking tour, or make arrangements with a walker with another car. In this case, the best arrangement is to drop one car off at the destination then car-pool to the starting point; another method is to meet the other walker/driver en route, switch car keys and then pick up the other car at the end to drive to some prearranged point to swap back again (a well thought-out plan is essential here!).

Due to the close-set network of routes on La Gomera, long-distance hikers will find good possibilities for treks with one or more overnight sojourns – among other choices, a walker can combine some of the routes suggested in this guide to create a four-to-seven day trek criss-crossing the island. Away from the tourist centres, however, not many overnight accommodations are available, so we recommend to pack at least a sleeping bag and bivouac shelter. Shopping possibilities en route are also often limited.

Walking on La Gomera

The most untamed of the Canary Islands

Like the other islands of the Canary archipelago, La Gomera is of volcanic origin. Despite its small area (369 km²), and its comparatively lower height (1487 m), the second smallest of the Canary Islands fuses a variety of landscapes into a compact space, with a range starting from the arid, desert-like south and stretching to the misty, tropical forested slopes of the central highlands. – Characteristic of La Gomera are the numerous gorges or ravines (*barrancos*), some plunging to depths of almost 800 m, blanketing the island like a web, its nucleus in the central highlands, spidering their way from there to the sea. Sometimes these have formed rugged, dramatic gorges, and sometimes gentle vales now blessed with picturesque terraces and palm tree groves. Wind-and-rain battered crags – the remains of volcanic plugs – can be found scattered throughout the entire island, but especially in the craggy playground of Los Roques (e.g. Roque de Agando).

Aeonium can be found on cliff walls and in the laurisilva forests.

Roque de Ojila and Roque de la Zarcita as seen from the Mirador del Bailadero.

Flora and Fauna

La Gomera claims many very different zones of vegetation depending on altitude and climatic conditions. Accordingly, the flora boasts of great variety, especially due to the endemic plants (growing naturally nowhere else but here on the island). In the coastal regions, mostly the moisture-conserving flora thrive, especially species of spurge (Euphorbia). In some valleys, banana trees can be seen – despite their comparative scarcity, bananas are one of the most important cash crops on the island. Many of the valley landscapes in the middle altitudes are characterised by the majestic palm trees (over 100,000 on the island) and particularly the Canarian date palm which can be found in altitudes up to 1300 m in the south. The renowned palm honey (Miel de Palma) is produced from the sap of the palm tree (*guarapo*). Not quite a quarter of the island's total area is covered by woodland; primarily thick laurel growth and Fayal-Brezal heath wood (laurisilva), that has established itself in the higher altitudes starting at about 600 m. The impressive laurel forest is the best-preserved of the entire Canary Islands – growing mostly on the damp northern and eastern slopes and in gorges. The Fayal-Brezel forests (heather trees and evergreen myrtle) thrive in the higher altitudes as well as the more arid zones. The broom-like Codeso shrub, sporting yellow flowers in early summer, are less wide spread as are the Canarian pine (especially on the southern-exposed slopes); these are very resistant to fire, surviving even the most devastating conflagration.

The only mammals frequently found in the mountains are rabbits and rodents. In the woods, you will often spot the laurel pigeon.

The National Park Visitor Centre Juego de Bolas.

National Park (Parque Nacional de Garajonay)

The Parque Nacional de Garajonay was established in 1981 and covers an area of about 10% (4000 hectares) of the island's total surface. The park's borders encompass a large part of the central highlands including Bosque del Cedro, which is considered the best-preserved and most pristine laurisilva (laurel) forest of the Canary archipelago and, for this reason, UNESCO declared the forest a World Cultural Heritage in 1986. It not only makes up the heart of the island, but also its »green lung« as well as its most important source of fresh water (for example, the Cedro Stream begins here and flows year-round). Not yet added to the national park region are the Enchereda chain and parts of the Cumbre Carbonera, although these also contain expanses of laurel forest worthy of conservation. – The national park is divided into numerous sheltered zones. Generally, all flora and fauna, but also the rock formations, are protected. In addition, straying from the official hiking trails or camping in the wild is forbidden by law. A brochure available from the National Park Administration contains specific information about the protective regulations in effect. At the National Park Visitor Centre Juego de Bolas (closed Mondays) on the main road Laguna Grande – Las Rosas, you can collect facts on the origins, geology, flora and fauna.

Beaches

Only a few beaches on La Gomera are suitable for swimming: Playa de San Sebastián (sand beaches on either side of the harbour), Playa de Avalo (partially sandy; north of San Sebastián), Playa de Santiago (only sandy at the harbour, otherwise – pebble beach), Playa del Medio (partially sandy, east of Santiago), Playa de Valle Gran Rey and Playa del Inglés near La Playa (partially sandy), Playa de Vueltas and Playa de las Arenas (both partially sandy, near Vueltas) and Playa de Alojera (lovely sandy bay). The island's north offers, aside from Playa de la Caleta (pretty partially sandy bay east of Hermigua) and the gravel beach Playa de Vallehermoso, only ocean-water swimming pools in Hermigua and at the Playa de Vallehermoso.

Botanical gardens

In Vallehermoso, on the main road to Playa, the Jardín Botánico del Descubrimiento. At the gardens of the National Park Visitor Centre Juego de Bolas – an interesting selection of Gomera's flora, especially that of the national park. In addition, delightful garden grounds at the Hotel Jardín Tecina (Playa de Santiago) and Finca de Argaga near Vueltas (fruit).

Canyoning

Some of the chasm-like, mostly dry-bed barrancos, present challenging gorge hikes. The most popular are the Barranco de Argaga and the Barranco de Arure.

Climbing

The island offers only a single climbing adventure – the Roque de Agando, 1250 m (about 200 m of rock face; a number of established routes IV–V). However, due to natural environment protection, climbing here is no longer allowed (since 1999). Other climbing routes are established on Roque El Cano and Roque Imada.

Excursions by boat

In Vueltas (Valle Gran Rey), but also in San Sebastián and Santiago, boat excursions can be taken to what is perhaps the island's greatest attraction: the organ pipe formations (Los Órganos).

Jeep Safaris

Jeep Safaris seem to prefer the tracks in the island's north.

Mountain-biking

This sport has gained much popularity, especially as a tourist amusement. The island offers ideal conditions for easy as well as for challenging excursions, especially along the forest trails and tracks of the national park and in the north. Bike rentals in San Sebastián, Santiago and Valle Gran Rey; also organised trips.

Museums

Centro de Visitantes Juego de Bolas near Las Rosas (exhibit and presentations concerning the national park; also workshops). In Hermigua, Museum Los Telares (ethnological museum, handicrafts).

Picnic places

Picnic places (Zona recreativa), supplied with tables and benches and usually also with barbecues, present a good target to use as a starting point or a finish for a walk – for example, Laguna Grande (this rest area also offers a large playground and a day tripper's restaurant), Chorros de Epina (excellent spring water, restaurant on the main road), Jardín de Las Creces, Raso de la Bruma, Ermita N.S. de Lourdes and Ermita Virgen de las Nieves.

Information and Addresses

Getting there

By air: La Gomera is only serviced by a regional airport near Playa de Santiago, that cannot be used by international flights (for example from mainland Europe). However, many flight connections exist to Tenerife-North and Gran Canaria.

By boat: Ferry connections between San Sebastián and Tenerife / Los Cristianos (frequent daily service by a number of lines, some with speed boats) as well as to La Palma and El Hierro. Also speed boat service Valle Gran Rey – Playa de Santiago – San Sebastián – Los Cristianos.

Tourist information

Patronato Insular de Turismo, Calle Real 4, San Sebastián de La Gomera, ℂ 922 14 15 12, 922 87 02 81, Fax 922 14 01 51.

Internet: Visit the Rother website at www.rother.de to find many useful links for La Gomera and the Canary Islands.

Camping

The only campsite is in El Cedro. Camping in the wild is not permitted.

Theft

Crime is a rare occurrence, however you should never leave valuables in your car or unguarded anywhere else.

Fiestas

The best-known fiestas are the Epiphany procession in Valle Gran Rey, Fiesta de San Marcos in Agulo (April 25), Fiesta Virgen del Carmen in Valle Gran Rey, Santiago and Vallehermoso (July 16) and Fiesta de la Virgen de Guadalupe in Puntallana near San Sebastián (October 5).

Climate

La Gomera enjoys a subtropical climate with slight variances in temperature between summer and winter. Most weather conditions are determined by the trade winds that bring wet and humid air masses from the north-east,

CLIMATE TABLE FOR LA GOMERA														
	Month	1	2	3	4	5	6	7	8	9	10	11	12	**Year**
Day	°C	20	20	21	22	23	25	27	29	27	25	23	21	24
Night	°C	15	15	15	16	16	18	20	22	21	20	17	17	18
Water	°C	19	19	19	19	20	21	22	23	23	22	22	21	21
Sunshine	(hrs)	5	6	7	8	9	10	11	10	8	6	6	5	8
Rainy days		11	8	6	5	2	1	0	1	2	6	8	8	5

Still a necessary stopover for most tourists visiting Gomera: the harbour of Los Cristianos, Tenerife.

collecting in the mountains and building up during the day to cover most of the island, especially the north, in a thick cloud cover.

Emergency phone numbers
International emergency call ☎ 112, Guardia Civil ☎ 062.

Taxi
All the major localities have a taxi stand. The fares are regulated, however, it is best to agree in advance on a charge to your destination.

	TIMETABLE FOR THE BUS ROUTES	
1	**SAN SEBASTIAN** – Peraza – Pajarito – Chipude – Arure – **VALLE GRAN REY (Vueltas)**	
	10.30, ■14.00, 17.30, ■21.30	■5.00, 7.30, ■12.30, ●14.00, ■16.00
2	**SAN SEBASTIAN** – Peraza – Santiago – **ALAJERO**	
	10.30, ■14.00, 17.30, ■21.30	■5.45, 8.15, ■12.45, ●16.00, ■17.00
3	**SAN SEBASTIAN** – Hermigua – Agulo – Las Rosas – **VALLEHERMOSO**	
	10.30, ■14.00, 17.30, ■21.30	■5.30, 8.00, ■13.00, 16.00
4	**ALOJERA** – Apartacaminos – **VALLEHERMOSO**	
	■7.00	■14.00
5	**VALLEHERMOSO** – Agulo – Hermigua – San Sebastián – Santiago – **AEROPUERTO**	
	■6.30, ■13.00	■8.30, ■17.30
6	**VALLE GRAN REY (Vueltas)** – Arure – Chipude – Alajeró – **AEROPUERTO**	
	■7.00, ■13.00	■9.00, ■17.30
7	**LA DAMA** – Chipude – Las Hayas – Apartacaminos – **VALLEHERMOSO**	
	■8.00	■13.00

Ask locally for up-to-date bus timeables on La Gomera (bus information ☎ 922 14 11 01)!
■ only Monday–Saturday, ● only Sunday

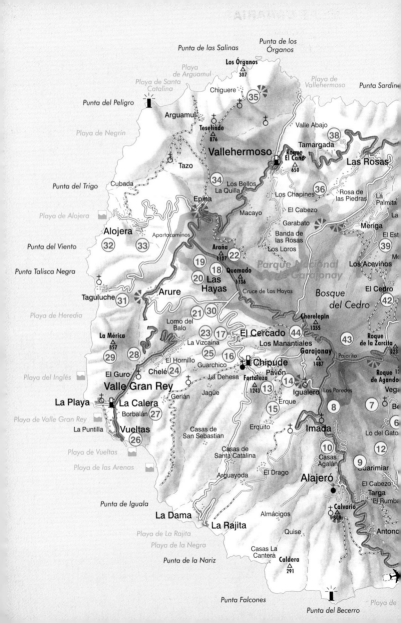

ISLAS CANARIAS

La Palma
Los Llanos 2426
Santa Cruz
Punta de
Fuencaliente
Cadiz
Isla Graciosa
671
Lanzarote
Playa Blanca Arrecife
Corralejo
La Gomera
1487
San Sebastián
Valverde
1500
El Hierro
La Laguna
Puerto
de la Cruz
Pico de Teide
3718
Tenerife
SANTA CRUZ
Granadilla
de Abona
Los
Cristianos
Agaete
**LAS
PALMAS**
1949
Maspalomas
Gran Canaria
Punta
de Jandía
625
807
Morro Jable
Gran Tarajal
**Puerto
del Rosario**
Fuerteventura

del Jurado

Agulo
Lepe
557
ana
al
La Caleta
40
ermigua
Las Nuevitas
Las Poyatas
El Convento
Enchereda
1065
Enchereda
41
Carretera del Norte
Lomo Fragoso
Chejelipes
a Laja
El Atajo
El Prado
El Jorado
El Molinito
San Antonio
y Pilar
Centr **Tagamiche**
933
Ayamosna
El Magro
4
Jerduñe
Playa de Hermigua
Punta Gabiña
Punta San Lorenzo
Playa de La Caleta
Playa de los Incendios
Tagaluche
Punta Palillos
Playa Molina
Punta Majona
Playa Majona
Casas de
Cuevas Blancas
2
Punta Gaviota
Playa Zamora
Playa del Aguila
Jaragán
642
Aluce
Punta Llana
Playa del Cangrejo
Punta de Avalo
Playa de Avalo
Punta de San Cristóbal
SAN SEBASTIÁN
de La Gomera
Playa de San Sebastián

Seima
5
El Cabrito
Casas de
Contrera
11
El Joradillo
Tejiade
Punta Gorda
Roque del Herrero
Playa de la Guancha
Playa de Machol
1
Playa de El Cabrito
Playa de Oroja
Playa de Suárez
Punta Gaviota
Playa del Medio
Playa de Santiago
a del Espino

The South-East Island

San Sebastián de La Gomera, Playa de Santiago and Alajeró

San Sebastián's city hall on the Plaza de Las Américas.

Gomera's south-east is characterised by barren slopes and dramatic, deep-cut *barrancos*. The least amount of precipitation falls here, especially in the sunny south around Playa de Santiago.

San Sebastián, the capital of the island with 5,000 inhabitants (about 30% of the approximately 17,000 total population) boasts the most historic events – even Columbus, the renowned »discoverer« of America, paused here during his overseas voyage. A tour of the city is best begun at the Plaza de Las Américas where the city hall (*ayuntamiento*) is located. Behind the spacious square, another square can be found: the Plaza de la Constitución with the former customs house (17th century; a Columbus fountain in the inner courtyard). Via the main shopping street, Calle del Medio, reach the church N.S. de la Asunción (1490 / 17th century), which is one of the oldest buildings on the island although the neighbouring Ermita de San Sebastián (15th century) is somewhat older (nearby, the Casa Colón – house number 56 with a small Columbus exhibit). The street running parallel, Calle Ruiz de Padrón, can be used to return to Plaza de Las Américas; on the way back, a detour to San Sebastián's landmark, the massive Torre del Conde (15th century), is worthwhile. If you prefer a longer tour, we recommend a climb to the *Parador* (10 min from the parish church). Next to the Monumento al Sagrado Corazón de Jesús on the main road heading south, enjoy the prettiest view overlooking the city.

Also, numerous interesting excursions can be made in the vicinity of San Sebastián: north of the city lies the lovely Playa de Avalo and the pilgrimage church Ermita Nuestra Señora de Guadalupe (16th century; every five years – a grand fiesta with a ship's procession). Also worthwhile is a visit to the idyllic »Valley of the Man-made Lakes« including the villages of Chejelipes and La Laja. The barren stretch between San Sebastián and Santiago is very attractive as well: abandoned villages and forsaken terraces are typical for the region once regarded as »the granary« of the island – an idyllic walker's paradise with solitary beaches only accessible by boat or hiking trails.

One of the most beautiful panoramic driving routes of the island is the main road heading toward Valle Gran Rey, passing by the Mirador Degollada de Peraza located in the national park and boasting the grand jubilee of crags Los Roques (Roque Agando, Zarcita, Ojila) and the fascinating laurel forest (laurisilva forest). Via the Cumbre de Tajaque reach the junction of Pajarito, a favourite starting point for the climb to Garajonay. The Carretera del Sur branches off from here heading south and winding downwards via Alajeró to **Playa de Santiago**. The up-and-coming seaside resort just adjacent to the new island airport boasts two nice beaches (Playa Santiago, Medio) and is an ideal starting point for walks in the romantic Benchijigua Valley and the rugged Guarimiar Gorge.

STARTING POINTS FOR WALKS

La Laja, 470 m

Palm grove village at the end of the road in the Barranco de la Villa (no bus service). Walking trails to Degollada de Peraza and Roque de Agando. From Lomito Fragoso y Honduras *caminos* to Cumbre Carbonera and to the Carretera del Norte at the turn-off of the track to Enchereda.

Mirador Degollada de Peraza, 951 m

Overlook and day-tripper's restaurant on the main road to Santiago or to Valle Gran Rey (bus stop for lines 1, 2 and 5). Walking trails to La Laja, San Sebastián, El Cabrito, Santiago and Roque de Agando.

Forest Fire Monument, 1073 m

Overlook directly at the foot of the Roque de Agando on the Carretera del Centro (bus stop for line 1). Walking trails to Benchijigua, Santiago, Imada and La Laja.

Pajarito, 1360 m

Road junction at the foot of Garajonay on the Carretera del Centro (bus stop for line 1). Walking trails to Garajonay and Imada.

Las Paredes, 1350 m

Road junction near Igualero on the mountain road (bus stop for lines 1 and 6). Walking trails to Garajonay, Imada, La Dama and Chipude.

Imada, 870 m / Alajeró, 843 m

Villages on or near the Carretera del Sur (bus stop for lines 2 and 6). Walking trails to Roque de Agando, Garajonay, Santiago, La Dama and into the dramatic Guarimiar Gorge.

Pastrana, 250 m / Guarimiar, 300 m

Idyllic villages at the end of the road in the Barranco de Santiago (no bus service). Walking trails to Imada, Alajeró and Roque de Agando.

1   From San Sebastián to Playa de la Guancha

Pleasant coastal walk to a solitary bay for a swim

San Sebastián – Playa de la Guancha (– Playa de El Cabrito) and back

Starting point: Seaside promenade near San Sebastián's city centre, 6 m (bus stop for lines 1, 2, 3, 5).
Walking time: San Sebastián – Playa de la Guancha 1¼ hrs, return 1¼ hrs; total time 2½ hrs.
Ascent: There and back about 200 m each way.
Grade: Short, easy walk with little ascent.
Refreshment: In San Sebastián.
Alternatives: From the Playa de la Guancha to Playa de El Cabrito: Past the solitary white house at the end of the beach, follow the trail which continues on, soon passing another white house. The

trail leads into the Barranco de la Guancha following the right-hand edge of the gorge. After about 10 min, pass under telephone posts then shortly after, the trail (white arrow on rock) changes over to the left valley flank and ascends bearing right soon reaching steep steps (watch for white markings; somewhat exposed) and after a good 10 m reach the crest of the mountain ridge, 147 m. The trail forks here – to the right, a possible descent to the Barranco Juan de Vera then via the Roque del Sombrero continuing to Degollada de Peraza (3¼ hrs from Playa de la Guancha, bus stop for lines 1, 2, 5; →Walk 5; hardy hikers could continue on from there via Walk 4 to return to San Sebastián) – however we take the left fork towards Playa de El Cabrito, traversing the slope and after a few minutes, above the hamlet El Cabrito, descend in zigzags to the stream bed of Barranco Juan de Vera. On the other side, reach a road that leads in a few minutes to Playa de El Cabrito (not quite 1 hr from Playa de la Guancha). From here, it is possible to continue the walk to Santiago (→Walk 11) or to Degollada de Peraza (→Walk 5).
Tip: Bring along your swimming gear!

The trail to Playa de la Guancha counts as one of the truly rare easy routes to be found on La Gomera. True, the route doesn't overwhelm the walker with spectacular scenery but nevertheless a lovely view of San Sebastián and Tenerife compensates for this. Also, a solitary, partially sandy beach presents a worthwhile goal and a suitable spot for a swim when the sea is fairly calm.

Follow the seaside promenade at **San Sebastián** heading south, then a good 100 m before it ends, turn right onto a street passing the UNELCO building. Immediately after, fork to the left and ascend an old *camino* along the slope above the UNELCO building and the beach. After a total of about

View of the Playa de la Guancha; the beach of El Cabrito juts out in the background – the coast trail continues on to there.

20 min, reach a solitary crucifix, 100 m, to enjoy a lovely view of the harbour and the city below – above us and to the right, we can see the Monumento al Sagrado Corazón de Jesús, which can be reached via an access road from the Carretera del Sur. The *camino* is distinct again, continuing on and bearing to the right. At first it leads almost on the level then ascends lightly traversing the slope above the steep coast, soon passing an old, circular threshing yard. A few minutes later, the ruins of a stone house appears to the left. Now the trail leads in a traverse into the Barranco del Revolcadero, only to climb back out again after crossing a road then bearing left and ascending lightly. After a good quarter hour, having left the *barranco* behind, cross over the high plain of El Veredal. Passing yet another threshing yard, the Playa de El Cabrito has already come into view. Shortly after, the **Playa de la Guancha** appears below. The *camino* now descends easily into a small *barranco* and then descends along this to the beach where a solitary, white house is standing. Passing the house, the trail continues to El Cabrito (→Alternative).

23

2 To the Casas de Cuevas Blancas

Diversified route to the remote »white caves«

Carretera del Norte, km 8 – Enchereda – La Gerode – Casas de Jaragán – Casas de Cuevas Blancas – La Gerode – Carretera del Norte, km 8

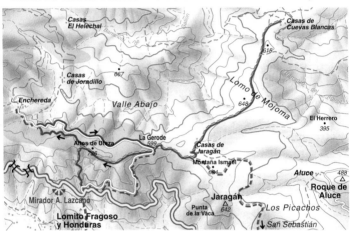

Starting point: Turn-off of the »Pista Forestal de Majona« from the Carretera del Norte, 430 m, near km 8 (bus lines 3 and 5).

Walking time: Carretera del Norte – Altos de Uteza – Enchereda 1 hr, Enchereda – La Gerode ½ hr, La Gerode – Casas de Jaragán 20 min, Casas de Jaragán – Casas de Cuevas Blancas 40 min, Casas de Cuevas Blancas – La Gerode 1 hr, La Gerode – Altos de Uteza – Carretera del Norte not quite 1 hr; total time 4½ hrs.

Ascent: A total of about 550 m.

Grade: Strenuous, briefly somewhat adventurous and precipitous route, mostly via good trails.

Alternatives: From Enchereda along the forestry road via Casas de Juel to Hermigua (about 5½ hrs along tracks; the delightful, old *camino* that, a few minutes after Enchereda, forks to the left in a gen-

tle valley notch and leads to the Enchereda summit, 1065 m, is closed to walkers to protect the natural environment). – **Descent from La Gerode to San Sebastián:** at the left-hand fork leading to the Casas de Jaragán, continue straight on and, after passing a cairn, bear left crossing the high plain of Jaragán, 642 m, through a small *barranco* and, on the other side, over the high plain of Lomo de las Nieves to descend to San Sebastián (3½ hrs from La Gerode). – **Descent from the Carretera del Norte to Lomo Fragoso:** directly across from the point where the forestry road merges into the main road, cross over the mining debris to reach the mountain ridge that extends into the Barranco de la Villa. Soon after, a *camino* descends to the right to reach the village (not quite ½ hr), from here descend along the valley road to end at San Sebastián (1 hr).

A short excursion leads to the Casas de Enchereda.

The Cuevas Blancas (»white caves«), carved by natural forces into beige-coloured outcrops of rock, belong to the most interesting geological features of the island. Despite the rather barren landscape of the eastern island, the route offers a remarkable scenic variety.

From the **Carretera del Norte**, ascend along the forestry road for about 50 m and then take a sharp turn to the left onto a wide, old *camino*. After a short ascent, we can already enjoy a lovely view into the Barranco de la Villa and also of San Sebastián and Roque de Agando; high above the ridge, a rock arch can be seen. The trail ascends easily for just under three quarters hour to reach a small saddle, 697 m, on the ridgeline of **Altos de Uteza**, and then forks.

To the right, a path leads along the south side of the ridge passing beneath the rock arch to continue to Gerode Pass (later our return route) – we take, however, the left fork which descends pleasantly at a good height to reach a forestry road in a good 10 min. A left turn here leads in 5 min to the dwellings of **Enchereda**, 600 m (goat pasturage). If you prefer not to take the detour, turn right to continue on the forestry road. This leads in easy up-and-down walking along the steep slope above the Barranco de Palopique, passing a pretty pine forest and heading straight towards a prominent needle rock with a huge cave. After half an hour roach the foot of the crag perched on the crest of the pass **La Gerode**, 599 m (the forestry road leads here after a sharp right-hand hook to the other side of the ridge descending to Carretera del Norte).

Turn left now onto an almost level *camino* that soon begins a somewhat steeper ascent, sometimes over ledges of rock, to reach a jutting rock

The ascent to the beautifully-situated Casas de Jaragán.

(5 min, nice place for break). Pass this to the right, following a light-coloured and somewhat precipitous ledge which leads beneath the huge cave piercing the rock needle. After a traverse of not quite 10 min, a somewhat indistinct and littered *camino* forks to the left (the main trail continues straight on towards San Sebastián). This ascends at first bearing slightly to the right, crosses below two houses to the left and finally climbs to the high spot to the left of the **Casas de Jaragán**, 680 m. Once at the top, enjoy a marvellous view – Tenerife seems only a stone's-throw away.

A detour to the highest point of the ridge, 710 m, can be made by turning left, but we follow the traces of the trail straight on over the high spot to reach the edge of a palm-dotted high valley, where a distinct, but stony *camino* descends bearing to the left. The *camino* passes between a stable and an old house with a tiled roof then crosses over to reach an old threshing yard (¼ hr from Casas de Jaragán). Cross over a small saddle, then again to the right of the ridgeline over a short stretch of light-coloured outcrop, reach a fork – here left, lightly ascending towards two large cairns. Arriving at the cairns, enjoy a view of Roque de Aluce and Playa de Avalo. Remain on the distinct path, ignoring the numerous cairns strewn all over the high plateau. Steadily walking along the ridge, we can soon see a drawn-out rocky ridge, sporting a beige-coloured outcrop of rock on the left flank, perforated with tiny caves. Our route follows this broad outcrop which presents a view into the dramatic Barranco de Majona. At the end, descend in a few minutes bearing slightly to the right to the **Casas de Cuevas Blancas**, 530 m. Near the houses, the largest and most interesting caves can be found – unfortunately so many watch dogs, some unchained, oppose the approach of strangers with such ferocity, that it is best to keep your distance.

After savouring a view of the steep, sheer cliff that marks the meeting of the Enchereda chain with the sea, return via the approach trail to the pass **La Gerode**. To avoid the following stretch of overgrown and toilsome trail, simply follow the forestry road descending left to the Carretera del Norte, however, we cross over the forestry road and ascend, bearing to the left, along the ridgeline without a distinct path (an easier ascent can made via the forestry road about 100 m further left, next to a palm tree). A faint path and cairns mark the way, leading along the ridgeline, sometimes through knee-high underbrush. Pass left below a crag to bear towards the dome behind which we can see the prominent rock arch that was already visible during the ascent. The trail leads at the dome along a beige-coloured outcrop and ascends bearing left over other outcrops to reach the left flank of the dome and then to skirt around the crag with the rock arch. After not quite half an hour of strenuous crossing, sometimes through thick underbrush, finally reach the saddle of **Altos de Uteza** and the approach trail; turn left to return to the **Carretera del Norte**.

Shortly before the Casas de Cuevas Blancas, the trail leads over a rock outcrop with numerous small caves.

3 From Degollada de Peraza to Roque de Agando

Exciting valley and high mountain walk within eyeshot of the Roques

Mirador Degollada de Peraza – La Laja – Degollada del Tanque – Carretera del Centro – Ermita Virgen de las Nieves – Mirador Degollada de Peraza

Starting point: Mirador Degollada de Peraza, 951 m, on the Carretera del Sur near km 16 (bus stop for lines 1, 2, 5).

Walking time: Mirador Degollada de Peraza – fork La Laja ¾ hr, fork – Degollada del Tanque a good 1 hr, Degollada del Tanque – Carretera del Centro 20 min, Carretera del Centro – Ermita Virgen de las Nieves 20 min, Ermita Virgen de las Nieves – Mirador Degollada de Peraza 25 min; total time 3 hrs.

Ascent: 700 m.

Grade: Via good *caminos*, an easy walk that nevertheless requires fitness due to the steep descent to La Laja and the long steady climb to the Carretera del Centro.

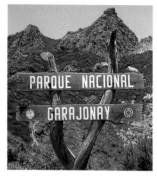

Refreshment: At the starting point – bar/restaurant Peraza. In La Laja – a small grocery store.

Alternatives: To avoid the descent to La Laja, simply begin the walk there. Also, by choosing the Carretera del Centro as the destination, the walk can end there (bus line 1).

Combination possible with with Walks 4–7.

Notice: The trail from Degollada del Tanque to Cruce de la Zarcita is closed to walkers to protect the natural environment.

The Roques come into view already during the descent to La Laja.

This grand circuit route, although somewhat strenuous, counts as one of the most popular of the island, and with just reason. The walk leads along marvellously designed old *caminos*, passing close to the craggy playground of »Los Roques« with Roque de Agando, Roque de la Zarcita and Roque de Ojila. While the descent to La Laja is extremely exposed to the sun, the continued route to the shelter at the Degollada del Tanque and to the picnic place next to the Ermita Virgen de las Nieves passes through stretches of delicious, shady pine forest.

Directly from the overlook platform of **Mirador Degollada de Peraza** (yellow markings) a steep, broad cobblestone trail winds down in a northerly direction into the Barranco de La Laja. During the descent through the southern-exposed sunshiny slope dotted with agave and palm trees, enjoy a fine view of Tenerife. Pass a few pines then the ruins of a stone house and after 20 min continue the descent straight on at a trail forking right (sign »La Laja«). A few minutes later, take a bend around the edge of a slope to see the houses of La Laja distinctly below. Before us, farther above at the valley head of Barranco de La Laja, the first *roques* appear. Subsequently in easy up-and-down walking cross over two gentle valley notches just below the timber line of the pine wood. After a total of three-quarters hour reach a jutting rock right above the village. Here the trail forks: straight on, a trail descends to **La Laja**, 470 m (leading in a few minutes to a cross with signs: then the trail bearing left returns to our route; straight on, a descent continues to the asphalt road on the other flank of the valley), but we bear left following the distinct yellow-marked trail leading directly along the edge of the wood and traversing the slope. Pass a dilapidated building and 10 min later the trail meets up with the main trail that approaches from the cross with signs. In a pleasant slope traverse, walk along for a few minutes above the village sporting evergreen cultivated terraces, then reach another fork. Here, turn left to ascend on the cobblestone trail (sign »Roque de Agando«), soon entering a sunny pine wood. Here and there, dead eucalyptus trees catch the eye – the remains of a devastating forest fire in 1984. For a short time, the trail ascends along a gentle valley floor then bears right along the slope. A splendid stretch follows along a cushion of pine needles crossing more gentle notches until the camino ascends again along the floor of yet another gentle valley. Pass a small dam wall then a few minutes later, reach a stone house perched on the upper edge of the forest, with benches protected from the wind – **Degollada del Tanque**, 853 m. Treat yourself to a break here and enjoy a glorious view of the Roques. A room in the simple hut is

The idyllic La Laja Valley.

The shelter on the Degollada del Tanque; in the background – Roque de Ojila.

open and can be used as an emergency shelter (sleeping bag essential). The route continues left of the hut and ascends pleasantly along a mountain ridge. Soon the last peak, the mighty Roque de Agando, appears in front of us. Our ever-ascending steadfast cobblestone *camino* aims directly, sometimes over steps, towards the high mountain road (Carretera del Centro) to finally reach this at the foot of Roque de Agando next to the sign »Parque Nacional Garajonay«. A short stretch to the right leads to a monument in memory of the forest fire: the Forest Fire Monument (car park, bus stop for line 1). We turn left, however, to follow the road for a good 100 m, then turn left again on the wide *camino* ascending in 20 min to the picnic place at **Ermita Virgen de las Nieves**, 1140 m. From the overlook platform in front of the chapel, enjoy a sweeping view of the southern island and Tenerife. Now follow the main road beneath the overlook platform to the left with a view of the bar/restaurant »Peraza«. 10 min later, just before the road bends to the right, fork to the left onto a smaller road. After another 10 min, a cobblestone *camino* forks to the left passing along a fenced property, then descends steeply to the traffic junction near the **Mirador Degollada de Peraza** – 100 m further on, reach the bar/restaurant of the same name.

4 From Degollada de Peraza to San Sebastián

Pleasant descent route with a constant view of Tenerife

Mirador Degollada de Peraza – Tagamiche – Ayamosna – San Sebastián

Starting point: Mirador Degollada de Peraza, 951 m, on the Carretera del Sur near km 16 (bus stop for lines 1, 2, 5).
Destination: San Sebastián, 6 m (bus stop for lines 1, 2, 3, 5).
Walking time: Bar/restaurant »Peraza« – Ayamosna a good 1 hr, Ayamosna – San Sebastián 1¾ hrs; total time 2¾ hrs.
Descent: 950 m.
Grade: All in all, an easy, mostly gradual descent, unfortunately often along a rather stony *camino*. Some perseverance is required.
Refreshment: At the starting point bar/restaurant »Peraza«. In San Sebastián

numerous bars and restaurants.
Alternatives: Sure-footed hikers in good physical condition may choose to extend the hike to a **circuit route**: from San Sebastián continue either along the main road farther on to La Laja and then ascend to Degollada de Peraza (about 3 hrs; →Walk 3) or – even nicer but very strenuous – via →Walk 1 to Playa de la Guancha and further on to El Cabrito, then ascending using →Walk 5 (in the reverse direction) via Roque del Sombrero to Degollada de Peraza (about 4 hrs).
Tip: Consider bringing your swimming gear along.

Although a bit monotonous and rather long, this exceptionally panoramic descent route with a constant view of Tenerife offers a pleasant walk. The route leads along one of the island's former main connecting trails, but is nevertheless not always well-maintained.

From the **bar/restaurant »Peraza«**, at first descend along the busy main road and then, after some minutes and after passing a fenced-in property, fork away left onto a road. Above us, we see a peak with a radio antennae perched on top: **Tagamiche**, 983 m, with a road ascending to the summit. Remain, however, on the small road bearing right and continuing above the main road. This skirts easily around Tagamiche. After a few minutes and in front of a power pylon, the road meets up with an old *camino* descending to

the right and immediately crossing the road a second time. The wide, some-what bumpy cobblestone trail bears to the left away from the pylons and after a few minutes of easy descent reaches a ridge. Along this bearing left and following beneath a long rock barrier, then passing below a stone house reach a gap with lovely views on the crest of the mountain ridge (½ hr from Peraza).

A path forks left here leading into the Barranco de la Villa. However, we remain on the *camino* ascending lightly along the right side of the ridge and pass Pico Gomero, 812 m. After about 10 min, the trail approaches the pylons again and then forks – take the left fork to continue with the pylons below. Immediately after, the trail passes above a dilapidated stone house and turns away again from the pylons. Gradually, we come to a broad high plain where soon a road descending from the left merges parallel to our *camino*. Take this road bearing left at the next fork (right El Magro), straight on over to the hamlet of **Ayamosna**, 690 m; the houses are built in the shelter of a rocky outcrop on the mountain ridge.

Below the first houses descend shortly to the right along a *camino* to reach the main trail that continues away from the ridge in a pleasant traverse. Soon San Sebastián appears, still far in the distance. Heading always towards the island's capital, descend over a barren, drawn-out mountain ridge. Soon reach a large fenced-in military zone protected by barking dogs, passing this directly on the left. About ½ hr from Ayamosna reach a road and continue the descent along this. Pass a solitary house then the road takes a bend around an old settlement with two stone houses and a threshing yard. Shortly before reaching a handful of white houses, fork right onto an old cobblestone trail. This descends steadily over a mountain ridge towards San Sebastián. In front of the first houses of the El Calvario district, a trail merges from the left then below a pump house bear left to descend to a street (Avenida de las Galanas) and continue along this. At the street's end turn left for a short stretch (the main road is to the right) and follow the

street Cañada del Herrero through the *barranco* descending to a bridge crossing the Barranco de la Villa. Following the *barranco* to the right, reach the nearby seaside promenade. Here left to reach the centre of **San Sebastián**.

5 From Degollada de Peraza to El Cabrito

Fascinating but strenuous circuit walk through the untamed, romantic south

Mirador Degollada de Peraza – Tagamiche – Ayamosna – El Magro – Roque del Sombrero – Playa de El Cabrito – Seima – (Jerduñe) – Mirador Degollada de Peraza

Starting point: Mirador Degollada de Peraza, 951 m, on the Carretera del Sur near km 16 (bus stop for lines 1, 2, 5).

Walking time: Mirador Degollada de Peraza – Ayamosna a good 1 hr, Ayamosna – El Magro ¾ hr, El Magro – El Cabrito 1¾ hrs, El Cabrito – Seima 1½ hrs, Seima – Mirador Degollada de Peraza 2 hrs; total time 7 hrs.

Ascent: 1000 m.

Grade: Strenuous circuit route requiring fitness and sure-footedness, mostly via narrow, little-used *caminos*. The stretch between El Magro and Roque del Sombrero might be blocked-off, however, it is officially open to walkers. From time to time, expect possible problems requiring some sense of direction.

Refreshment: Bar/restaurant »Peraza« at the starting point.

Possible combinations: From El Cabrito a continuation possible to San Sebastián (2¼ hrs; →Walks 1 and 11). From Seima, a continuation possible to Santiago (a good 3 hrs; →Walk 11).

Tip: Don't forget your swimming gear!

What a walk! One highlight after another in a region where you would least expect it: quaint, often abandoned villages, savage gorges, bizarre crags, ingeniously constructed trails and last, but not least, the garden oasis of El Cabrito sporting a lovely, inviting beach – perfect for a swim when the waters are quiet. However, stamina is required for walkers tackling this barren, untamed plot of God's earth.

From **Mirador Degollada de Peraza** follow the route described in Walk 4 until reaching the fork shortly before the hamlet **Ayamosna**, 690 m. (The former route that descends directly from Tagamiche to Roque del Sombrero has unfortunately been closed to hikers by official order due to pressure brought about by the local stock breeders). At the fork, we leave Walk 4 behind by turning right onto the road leading over to **El Magro**, 690 m, located on the main road.

On the other side of the main road, a *camino* continues, descending and bearing right into the Barranco de la Guancha. The old trail is somewhat overgrown and after a quarter hour reaches a flat ridge above the *barranco* floor – here, (in front of a level area) bear right at the fork, cross over a small side valley and reach the stream bed of the *barranco* at about the same altitude (5 min). Ascend for about 20 m along the *barranco* then continue along the trail by turning sharply left and ascend along the other valley flank to Roque de Magro (soon cross a stone barrier by scrambling over). After a quarter hour, always keeping to the main trail, the now broader *camino* leads beneath the cliff wall of Roque de Magro passing a few palm trees. 5 min later, on the ridgeline reach the old abandoned settlement **El Magro**.

Here meet the former trail that continues to the left along the ridge to the saddle in front of **Roque del Sombrero**, 672 m; skirt around to the right of this crag »hat«. Afterward, continue along the ridgeline to the next group of crags marked by extreme erosion at the base. From the saddle at the foot of the crag cluster, the trail descends to the right in zigzags, soon passing palm trees then continuing directly along the foot of the crags – a fascinating stretch! After a quarter hour, we have skirted around the crags and then, once again walking along the ridgeline, reach a solitary house. Descending further along the ridgeline, reach the rocky crag **Roque García**, 443 m. Skirt the first crags to the left, then make a short ascent with a dazzling downward view of the dramatic Barranco de la Guancha to reach a small saddle. From here, a short descent to the right, then left over an outcrop with a dizzying view down into the Barranco Juan de Vera leading over to a rock platform –

The beach at El Cabrito – one of the highlights of the walk through the southern island.

an overlook par excellence where we can already see El Cabrito before us. Continue along the outcrop beneath a beautiful basalt cliff wall, then in a few minutes, near a small crag shaped like a surreal hand, once again reach the crest of the ridge. A few metres past the »stone hand«, 304 m, the path turns to the right descending in steep zigzags with scree underfoot to the Barranco Juan de Vera (at the end, bear somewhat to the right). The arduous descent lasts for about 20 min. At the end cross over to the floor of the *barranco* and follow the trail on the right edge of the gorge descending into the valley. Before El Cabrito, continue along the gravel road to the left following a wall while skirting around this vast terrain detached from the outside world (soon a *camino* forks left crossing the floor of the *barranco* leading to Playa de la Guancha and continuing on to San Sebastián). After a total of about 40 min reach the broad pebble beach of **Playa de El Cabrito**.

Now follow the road that leads between the seaside resort and the beach until soon reaching the boat landing (here some sandier beach). Now turn to the right following the road into the valley, leading between a cliff face and the gardened grounds of the exclusive residential estate founded by the Viennese artist Otto Mühl. Right after, a *camino* flanked by small walls turns to the left (yellow-numbered) which we leave again in front of a housing complex by taking a left onto a steeply ascending cobblestone trail. After a few minutes of ascent, bear left at a fork, then shortly after to the right. The *camino* climbs quickly, opening a lovely view of El Cabrito. After a total of about 30 min reach the ridgeline and ascend further along this. After the power pylon, the pleasant trail leads a bit to the left away from the ridge, returning however in not quite half an hour – here, a *camino* merges from the right out of the Barranco Juan de Vera, and an interesting overview of our approach route to El Cabrito can be examined from this point. During the further ascent through the dreary terraced slope enjoy backwards views of the Playa de la Guancha and Tenerife. After about 10 min, the *camino* levels out and leads in a traverse, presenting a view of Santiago and the airport, then continues straight on to the nearby houses of the abandoned settlement **Seima**, 530 m.

At first, the trail passes below a group of houses with a large, old stone baking oven then shortly after, another group of houses. After the last house, a *camino* forks left to the Casas de Contrera and continues towards Santiago, but we remain on the trail continuing straight on. During the ascent on the *camino*, which has deteriorated and lost distinctness, pass by other properties and head directly toward a prominent crag crowned by a power pylon, at the foot of which, bear left to continue the ascent. Subsequently, the trail leads parallel to the wooden pylons (after 10 min, above a property, a *camino* merges from the left ascending from the Casas de Contrera), then finally arrives at an idyllic, palm-dotted high valley, dipping down into this while opening a view of the Barranco de Chinguarime and Santiago. Shortly after, bearing right, pass through a lovely-situated and abandoned hamlet – some of the houses are built into the crags of Alto de Tacalcuse. Here's a pretty place to rest and explore! Right after the houses, scramble over a rockslide (a spring just below) and continue the hike into the *barranco* over a plate of rock. In steady up-and-down walking, pass below surreal rock formations right at the edge of Barranco de Chinguarime – a stunning contrast to the barren high plains that we have just left behind. Now it takes a very long time for the trail to level out and then, after a good half hour, pass above a few houses at a saddle (to the right, a possible descent into the Barranco Juan de Vera, across from the bar/restaurant »Peraza«). Continuing the ascent along the *camino* for some minutes more, arrive at a hairpin bend to reach the old Carretera del Sur (to the left, a continued walk to reach **Jerduñe**, 800 m). Turn right here and then right again to continue along the new Carretera del Sur. Along this and accompanied by tiresome traffic, return easily to the starting point, **Mirador Degollada de Peraza**, in a good 20 min.

6 From Roque de Agando to Santiago

Popular descent through a picturesque valley

Forest Fire Monument at Roque de Agando – Benchijigua (– Lo del Gato) – Pastrana – Taco – Playa de Santiago

The Carretera del Centro passes directly at the foot of the Roque de Agando.

Starting point: Forest Fire Monument, 1073 m, on the Carretera del Centro, directly at the foot of Roque de Agando (bus stop for line 1).

Destination: Playa de Santiago, 10 m (bus stop for lines 2, 5).

Walking time: Forest Fire Monument – Benchijigua 1 hr, Benchijigua – Pastrana 1¼ hrs, Pastrana – Taco ¼ hr, Taco – Playa de Santiago not quite 1 hr; total time 3½ hrs.

Descent: 1100 m.

Grade: At first a very steep, later a mostly pleasant descent route via cobblestone trails; at the end via a lightly-travelled road (4 km).

Refreshment: In Playa de Santiago several bars and restaurants.

Combination possible with Walks 3, 7, 9 and 12.

Tip: You might want to bring your bathing gear along.

The descent from Roque de Agando to Playa de Santiago is one of the most spectacular, classic walks on Gomera. The route leads through a picturesque high mountain valley, blanketed in pine forest and flanked by plunging cliff walls, descending into the superbly-situated hamlet Benchijigua. Equally lovely is the final stretch to reach the heavenly palm tree garden at Pastrana. Only the »finale«: the trudge along the main road to Santiago isn't exactly a cup-of-tea for most walkers, however a dip in the Atlantic at the

Playa de Santiago can well compensate for this.

Behind the terrace walls at the **Forest Fire Monument**, a stone-paved *camino* begins, immediately descending steeply along the slope and then, taking a slight bend, continues towards the valley. It leads constantly along the left flank of the *barranco*, at first through pines then through low scrubby woodland. After a quarter hour pass below the foot of the cliff Roque de Agando then, 10 min later, the *camino* crosses over a large, covered water channel and immediately after, the stream bed. Now on the right flank of the valley begin an easy descent in a steady traverse heading toward the hamlet of Benchijigua already in view. After a total of about 50 min, just above the settlement, meet up with a lovely, old water distributor. Pass this to the left continuing the descent and then bear right in front of the next water distributor. Left at the next fork, descend to the grand *plaza* of **Benchijigua**, 610 m (bar) – a splendid place for a good, long break enhanced by a very fine view of the high mountain valley which we have just left behind and the spectacular craggy tower Roque de Agando. Even more commanding is the view from the mini-*mirador*, which can be reached via a short ascent starting from the chapel only 150 m away.

Continue to the left on the track road, then after about 100 m turn right onto the *camino* soon leaving the last houses of the hamlet behind, bearing slightly left and grad-

Benchijigua – backwards view of the high valley at the foot of Roque de Agando.

ually leading over to the left flank of the valley (always remain on the main trail!). After a quarter hour, the *camino* crosses over the *barranco* floor and then shortly after meets a road descending to Lo del Gato. Ascend along this about 100 m to the left to the next left-hand bend. From here, our *camino* continues to the right, after a few minutes leading through a terrain of black sand (bearing left) and then, soon afterwards, crossing two lovely side valleys one after the other. About 20 min from the road, a *camino* forks right to Lo del Gato (→Walk 12). Remain on the trail leading straight on and continuing above the floor of the Barranco de Benchijigua towards the valley. Only after another 20 min from the road and after traversing along a cliff face, the trail descends, passing the ruins of a house as well as two water reservoirs, to the *barranco* floor. Another 50 m along the floor, pass an old *gofio* (grain) mill still in use. About 50 m after the mill, the trail leaves the *barranco* floor by bearing left; after a short ascent along the slope the trail passes above cultivated terraces. We find ourselves in the middle of a fabulous grove of pine trees surrounding the village of **Pastrana**, 250 m, and then meet up with a street ending here near the first houses.

The shortest and easiest route is to descend along the street, but you could also, about 100 m on, shortly before a large water pipe crosses over the street, take a sharp right onto a descending *camino* that passes above a transformer then descends to the *barranco* floor. Here, along the track then along the asphalt street continuing down the valley. In the hamlet of **Taco**, 200 m, a street coming from Pastrana merges from the left. Now continue descending in the valley, crossing the newly-built Carretera del Sur to reach **Playa de Santiago**. Right onto the old main road, reach the village centre where the harbour and the beach are not far away.

Playa de Santiago as seen from the hotel »Jardin Tecina«.

7 From Pajarito to Roque de Agando

Impressive but strenuous high mountain walk

Pajarito – Imada – El Azadoe – Benchijigua – Forest Fire Monument at Roque de Agando

Starting point: Road junction at Pajarito, 1360 m, on the Carretera del Centro, at the foot of Garajonay (bus stop for line 1).

Destination: Forest Fire Monument, 1073 m, on the Carretera del Centro, directly at the foot of Roque de Agando (bus stop for line 1).

Walking time: Pajarito – Imada 1¾ hrs, Imada – El Azadoe ¾ hr, El Azadoe – Benchijigua not quite 1 hr, Benchijigua – Forest Fire Monument 1¼ hrs; total time 4¾ hrs.

Ascent: 600 m and 900 m in descent.

Grade: Strenuous, a high mountain hike with stretches of steep ascents and descents that require sure-footedness.

Refreshment: Bars in Imada and Benchijigua.

Combination possible with Walks 6, 8, 9, 12, 13, 14 and 44.

Tip: The walking route can also start in Imada (bus stop for line 2 on the Carretera del Sur, from there, 25 min by foot to reach the village).

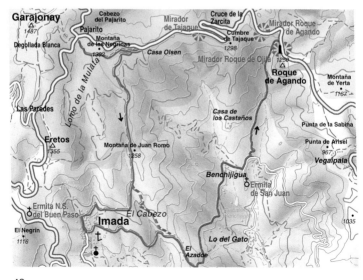

The first leg of the walk: the descent to Imada passes via the Olsen hut (photo page 42).

This high mountain walk leads in steady up-and-down walking with excellent views of the southern island and especially of the Roque de Agando, touching on two of the most picturesquely-situated hamlets on Gomera – Imada and Benchijigua. But – no sweet without sweat – the route requires good physical fitness, especially due to the steep final ascent to Roque de Agando. In addition, the stretch between El Azadoe and Benchijigua is poorly-maintained and somewhat overgrown.

From the car park on the road junction at **Pajarito** follow the forestry road leading in a southerly direction into the pine forest (sign »Los Roques«). Not quite 5 min on, a distinct, signed forest trail forks left, then shortly afterwards steeply ascends to a hill with a phenomenal view sweeping over the vast forests of Bosque del Cedro and Garajonay, with the Roque de Agando thrusting out of the hilly landscape. Crossing over another hill, descend bearing left (after 5 min ignore the left fork leading to the main road) to finally reach the Carretera del Centro. 50 m on, take a sharp right onto a forestry track. To the left and above us, we can see the **Olsen hut**, 1330 m, a small, squat block of cement with an antennae and another track passing by it (20 min from Pajarito, lovely panoramic view).

Taking the right-hand forestry track, cross through laurel woods later mixed with pine to reach a ridgeline (always follow the track descending straight on). A good 20 min after the Olsen hut, the wide forestry track hooks sharply to the right. Straight ahead on the narrow ridgeline, a broader trail continues (sign »Imada«) and then becomes a *camino* shortly after. This leads on the level at first then descends the slope to the right of the ridgeline and forks after not quite a quarter hour at a jutting rock – at this point, the high valley dissolves rapidly into a *barranco*. Bear right through the valley floor (to the left, a direct descent to El Azadoe, about ¾ hr shorter than via Imada) and traverse to a small mountain spur for a first view of Imada. Always bearing right, descend along the slope to enjoy a lovely view sweeping over the dramatic Barranco de Guarimiar to Santiago. After crossing a small *barranco* just before the village, the *camino* passes above cultivated terraces to reach the first house and then merges into a street. Along this and passing a turn-about with a bar/café (right) and a school/telephone booth (left), descend to the lowest point of the street to **Imada**, 870 m.

Here descend to the left over stairs and then immediately follow the intersecting trail to the left, leaving the village then crossing two stream beds one after another. After the second, larger stream bed, ascend to a red rock ridgeline, sometimes over steps, and pass a final house (¼ hr from Imada). From here enjoy another pretty view of Imada. Continue on a pleasant high walk, sometimes crossing over beige-coloured outcrops of rock. After 15 min pass above some abandoned houses – here at the fork descend to

The Cumbre de Tajaque fixes the setting during the ascent to Agando.

the right (passing to the left of the houses). In front of us, we can already see the hamlet of **El Azadoe**, 830 m; reach the ruins of the houses after crossing the *barranco* of the same name (along this stretch, the short cut skirting the jutting rock merges from the left).

Above the houses and at a gap, reach the crest of the mountain ridge (left above a mushroom-shaped crag next to an old threshing yard – from here, a good overview of the continued route to Benchijigua and to Roque de Agando). Our route descends on the other side of the ridgeline bearing right along the slope and forks after a few minutes – here turn left onto the narrow, somewhat bumpy and overgrown path descending in tight zigzags (the level trail straight on – a descent possible to El Cabezo, →Walk 12). After a good

Idyllic Nature at the trail's edge.

quarter hour, the trail bends a bit to the left towards a solitary, light-coloured building, to pass above this a few minutes later. In a steady traverse of the slope, with a downwards view of Lo del Gato, the trail continues until merging into a road above a stone wall. The road leads in a few minutes to the *plaza* of **Benchijigua**, 610 m (bar), where a number of roads meet (to the left, reach the chapel 150 m on, where you can ascend to the left to a miniature *mirador*).

We continue along the road by turning left and then, 20 m on, turn right only to turn right again after another 20 m onto the ascending *camino*. 150 m on, in front of a grove of eucalyptus trees, fork again to the right. Cross a small water channel then turn left to climb to a height with a water channel and a water distributor (a lovely spot for a break with a view of Roque de Agando). The trail continues at first ascending the ridgeline then bears right in a long traverse entering the delightful high valley at the foot of Roque de Agando. About 20 min after leaving the height, cross over a *barranco* then immediately after, a covered water channel. Along the right valley flank, passing below Roque de Agando, begin a steep ascent. Soon reach a shady pine wood and finally, after climbing steep steps, arrive at the **Forest Fire Monument** on the high mountain road (Carretera del Centro).

8　From Pajarito via Imada to Garajonay

Panoramic circuit route to the island's highest peak

Pajarito – Imada – Las Paredes (– Igualero) – Garajonay – Pajarito

Starting point: Road junction at Pajarito, 1360 m, on the Carretera del Centro at the foot of Garajonay (bus stop for line 1).

Walking time: Pajarito – Imada 1¾ hrs, Imada – Las Paredes 1 hr, Las Paredes – Garajonay not quite ¾ hr, Garajonay – Pajarito 20 min; total time 3¾ hrs.

Ascent: 650 m.

Grade: Except for the steep ascent from Imada, mostly pleasant mountain walk via good trails.

Refreshment: Bar in Imada.

Combination possible with Walks 7, 9, 13, 14 and 44.

Tip: The walk can also begin in Imada (bus stop for line 2 on the Carretera del Sur, from there 25 min by foot to the village).

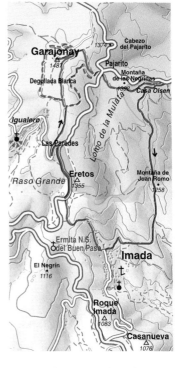

This circuit route belongs to the most panoramic walks of this guide – aside from the celebrated Garajonay overlook, the route offers time and again sweeping views of the island's south. The walk also touches on pretty pine forests.

From the car park on the road junction at **Pajarito** begin following Walk 7 via the **Olsen hut** to **Imada**, 870 m. Here, descend along the asphalt village street to a large turnabout with a bar/café (right) and a telephone booth and a school (left). Now return about 50 m along the street (ascending) until a broad *camino* forks to the left. This climbs steeply and after not quite a quarter hour crosses a water channel next to a little house (to the right of the channel – a water tunnel). The trail crosses gradually to the left flank of the valley then ascends lightly bearing left to a mountain spur with a sweeping view over the Barranco de Guarimiar to Santiago (½ hr from Imada). Now a final steep ascent, not quite 10 min long, to reach the crest of the mountain ridge. To the left, we can see the main road ascending

Imada, one of the prettiest-situated villages on Gomera.

from Santiago, but remain on the *camino* that passes to the left of a little house then shortly after, in front of a prominent block of rock, 1312 m, merges with the main road. Ascend along this for about 10 min to the road junction at **Las Paredes**, 1350 m (bus stop for lines 1, 6).

Here turn left on the road towards Chipude but immediately leave it again at the next bend by forking right onto an ascending forestry trail (sign »Garajonay«). To the left in the valley, Igualero, the island's highest village appears – behind it, a *mirador* of the same name sporting a chapel and also the Fortaleza can be seen. After 10 min ascent – always climbing straight along the forestry trail – meet a broad intersecting track (to the right a possible descent to the road junction at Pajarito, 20 min). Follow this track 30 m to the left then bear right onto another forestry trail. This crosses a hilltop 5 min later then leads pleasantly along the slope and after a total of 15 min reaches a saddle (1448 m) with a major trail junction. Here left along the ridge trail climbing in a good 5 min to the platform on the peak of **Garajonay**, 1487 m.

After a well-deserved break, return to the **saddle** (1448 m) but now remain on the ridge trail leading straight on and ascending shortly then reach a fork after 3 min (sign »Garajonay/Contadero«, 1463 m). Turn right here onto the steep, stepped trail to descend in a good 10 min to the road junction at **Pajarito** (after a good 5 min, a stretch of ascent).

9 Barranco de Guarimiar

Spectacular walk through the Guarimiar Gorge

Imada – Guarimiar – Targa – Alajeró – Imada

Starting point: Imada, 870 m (bus stop for lines 2 and 6 on the Carretera del Sur at the turn-off of the access road towards Imada – from there 25 min by foot).

Walking time: Imada – Guarimiar 1 hr, Guarimiar – Targa – Alajeró 20 min, Alajeró – Imada ¾ hr; total time 3¾ hrs.

Ascent: 750 m.

Grade: The walk always follows good, sufficiently broad cobblestone trails but nevertheless requires a lot of stamina as well as sure-footedness and an excellent head for heights, especially during the strenuous steep ascent to Targa.

Refreshment: In Alajeró bar/restaurant, in Imada bar.

Alternatives: Begin the walk in Taco or in Guarimiar: From Santiago, walk along the main road towards Pastrana until reaching the fork in Taco (4 km). Continuing straight on along the valley road, reach the hamlet of Guarimiar at the road's end (here left ascending through the *barranco* to reach the trail) – the route via El Rumbazo is even nicer: only a few minutes after Taco, a street forks left to cross over the first bridge into El Rumbazo. Directly in front of the first houses, turn right onto a *camino* that ascends steadily into the valley and, 20 min from Taco, forks at a stone house (to the right, the route continues to Guarimiar; left – an ascent to Targa). – From Guarimiar, a possible descent to Santiago (1¼ hrs). – From Targa, a possible descent to Antoncojo and then further on to Santiago (1¼ hrs).

Combination possible with Walks 6, 7, 8, 10 and 12.

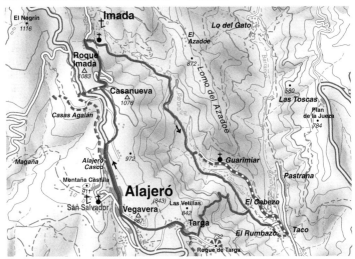

The route through the Guarimiar Gorge leads along the foot of a mighty cliff.

This ingeniously constructed *camino* through the Barranco de Guarimiar is without a doubt one of Gomera's most spectacular walking routes. It leads directly along the dizzying, sheer cliff wall of the chasm-like gorge (hundreds of metres deep) to descend to Guarimiar. Nevertheless, the climax of the walk is the breathtaking ascent to Targa – easily comparable to a crag-viewing route in the Alpine Dolomites. This circuit route is also targeted to the car-hire walker – following *caminos* and roads back to Imada. Those making the approach by public bus, may choose to finish the walk in Targa or Alajeró.

Begin the walk at the lowest point of the village street in **Imada**, directly where the street begins a steep ascent. Here, turn right onto the stepped trail, then bear immediately right at the fork (to the left, the trail continues towards El Azadoe). Below the last houses, the trail becomes a narrow *camino*, passes cultivated terraces and leads to the right to join the main trail that descends pleasantly along the right flank of the valley and passes a dilapidated house after a quarter hour. Gradually, we leave the gentle, terrace-cultivated high mountain valley of Imada behind us and enter into the Guarimiar Gorge, flanked by dramatic sheer cliffs. About half an hour from Imada, reach a small mountain spur with a rock platform and from here descend in steep bends. The hamlet of Guarimiar, marking the first stage of our route, already appears before us. Now begins what is perhaps the most breathtaking stretch of the walk: along natural ledges of rock with dizzying downward views of the narrow gorge, the trail descends steadily and lightly along the foot of bizarre, sometimes overhanging, cliff walls. After a total of three-quarters' hour, meet a large water channel to cross over this to the left then continue the descent to reach **Guarimiar**, 300 m.

In front of the first house of the pretty little hamlet with cultivated terraces and palm trees, perched at the end of the sheer-walled gorge, a *camino* descends to the left of the *barranco* floor reaching a road nearby that follows the left flank of the valley via Taco to Santiago. Instead, we turn right then continue, passing to the left of the first house and remaining on the *camino* which leads along the slope of the right-hand flank of the valley. After 5 min ignore a short cut forking to the right and a quarter hour later the *camino* forks again above the ruins of a stone house; here continue to the right

Dizzying downward view into the depths of the gorge.

(from the left, a trail from El Rumbazo merges, →Alternative). The *camino* to Targa ascends for a few minutes towards a small, palm-dotted gentle valley notch then leads to the right climbing farther along the steep slope with lovely views of the Barranco de Guarimiar and El Cabezo. Still climbing, cross over a water channel. Never very exposed, the always sufficiently broad trail ascends over outcrops and through gullies to reach a reddish-coloured saddle on the ridgeline and finally meets a road (follow this to the left for 10 min to reach a magnificent overlook/survey point with a fantastic view of Santiago and the airport). We turn right onto the road (30 m on, next to an old threshing yard, a *camino* forks to the left towards Antoncojo) and shortly after, in **Targa**, 740 m, turn right onto the asphalt road (to the left – the Carretera del Sur, bus stop for lines 2 and 6).

Panoramic view from Guarimiar of the gorge's plunging cliffs.

The road climbs in bends. After a few minutes and past the last left-hand bend above the village, reach a small height and immediately after passing a quarry, turn right onto a broad cobblestone trail that soon passes the first houses of Alajeró. This forks 5 min later at an old, circular threshing yard – here continue by turning right towards the village centre. To the left, enjoy a view of Calvario with the neighbouring island of El Hierro behind. Across from the bar/restaurant »Las Palmeras« (bus stop for lines 2 and 6) reach the rather busy main road to ascend along this passing through **Alajeró**, 843 m. After a good quarter hour reach a junction: a street forks to the left towards the church in the village centre; straight on, parallel to the Carretera del Sur, a wide *camino* continues – here a detour to the dragon tree of Agalán can be made (→Walk 10). We remain on the main road only to leave it again at the next left-hand bend by turning right onto the broad *camino* which ascends above the road. After a good 10 min, on the ridgeline, meet the access road that leads to Imada; here descend to the right along a *camino* that short-cuts the wide bends in the road and finally reaches **Imada** (not quite 20 min; by the way, below Roque de Imada, the old connecting trail to Guarimiar forks away to the right).

Jan 07 - a lut of a clammer - but good paths & steps

10 To the Dragon Tree of Agalán

Short excursion to Gomera's largest dragon tree

Cruce de Imada – Drago – Casas de Agalán (– Calvario) – Cruce de Imada

Location: Alajeró, 843 m, Imada, 870 m.
Starting point: Car park 200 m above Cruce de Imada (junction from the main road to Imada from the Carretera del Sur, bus stop for lines 2, 6); about 1 km above Alajeró.
Walking time: Cruce de Imada – *drago* ½ hr, return a good ½ hr; total time 1 hr.
Ascent: 150 m.
Grade: Short, easy walk – however at the end, the path is steep and stony leading through a field of cactus.
Refreshment: Only in Alajeró.
Alternative: The ascent to Calvario, 808 m: on the return route, a good 5 min after Agalán (see below), turn right onto

Chapel on the crest of Calvario.

the broad *camino* which descends to a road junction. Here right again onto the village street to descend to Alajeró's church. From here continue the descent along the street and turn left at the next crossing then after 100 m, in front of the bar/restaurant »Columba« turn right to descend along another street. Not quite 10 min from the church square reach a fork to turn left descending to the foot of Calvario. Here take a broad cobblestone trail to climb to the crest of the peak with the Ermita San Isidro and a picnic place. Now enjoy a superlative view of the southern island (from the church square at Alajeró 1 hr, there and back; from the detour during the drago walk, add another hour).
Combination possible with Walk 9.

Unlike Tenerife and La Palma, dragon trees are an absolute botanical rarity on La Gomera. The only state-owned »drago« is growing in a picturesque *barranco* surrounded by fig cactus and agave near Agalán and somewhat above Alajeró.

The magnificent dragon tree of Agalán.

10 m below the **car park**, a *camino* flanked by small stone walls forks off in a right angle from the main road (Carretera del Sur). This descends in a bend and in not quite 10 min crosses a road coming from Agalán. Shortly after, the *camino* forks: straight on reach an overlook platform with a view of the dragon tree, to the left, the route continues towards the *drago*. This ends after a quarter hour at a platform in front of the spacious, fenced-in area around the **Drago**.

Now return via the *camino* until reaching the road (20 min) to turn to the right. About 200 m on, pass to the left of the houses of **Agalán** and then follow the street to the left (soon reach a striking threshing yard on the right). After a good 5 min and shortly before the main road, a broad, stone-paved *camino* crosses the street (to the right, a possible descent to Alajeró and to Calvario, →Alternative). Turning left and parallel to the main road, return to the **car park**.

11 From Santiago to San Sebastián

Long, hard hike to the isolated beaches on the southern coast

Playa de Santiago – Playa del Medio – El Joradillo – Casas de Contrera – Seima – Playa de El Cabrito – Playa de la Guancha – San Sebastián

Starting point: Hotel Tecina, 90 m (bus stop for lines 2, 5), in Santiago, 10 m.

Destination: San Sebastián, 6 m (bus stop for lines 1–3, 5).

Walking time: Hotel Tecina – Playa del Medio ½ hr, Playa del Medio – Contrera 2 hrs, Contrera – Seima a good ¾ hr, Seima – El Cabrito 1¼ hrs, El Cabrito – Playa de la Guancha not quite 1 hr, Playa de la Guancha – San Sebastián 1¼ hrs; total time 6¾ hrs.

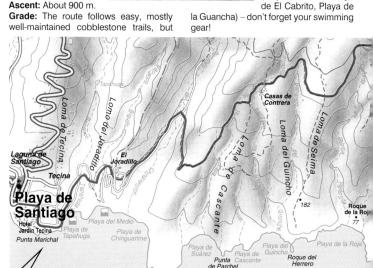

Ascent: About 900 m.

Grade: The route follows easy, mostly well-maintained cobblestone trails, but nevertheless requires physical fitness as well as a good sense of direction. No shade – very hot!

Refreshment: Bar/restaurants in Santiago and in San Sebastián.

Alternative: Most walkers only make it as far as the lovely Playa del Medio (½ hr one-way).

Combination possible with Walk 5.

Tip: Choice swimming spots on the route (Playa del Medio, Playa de El Cabrito, Playa de la Guancha) – don't forget your swimming gear!

This long, pitiless trudge above the barren southern coast, crossing through *barrancos* again and again is by no means a piece of cake. In former times, a multitude of terraces were established here, but today the route leads past often abandoned, sometimes seemingly ancient, ruins of hamlets. Only the verdant oasis of El Cabrito and the inviting beach bays hearten the walk.

From the bus stop on the main road, turn onto a side street that passes above the **Hotel Tecina**. Immediately past the spacious bungalow grounds turn right on the track road that hooks to the left and at the same time leads along the steep coast and then drops into the Barranco de Tapahuga where a track forks to the right leading to **Playa de Tapahuga**. However, remain on the dusty track road, frequented by tourist traffic to the beach, that climbs to the next mountain ridge (a short cut is possible via an old cobblestone trail). The **Playa del Medio** appears below, one of the island's prettiest beach bays, accessible by turning right onto a steep, scree-covered path. Remaining on the track, however, descend into the Barranco Biquillo, where another track turns to the right towards the beach. Here, at the floor of the *barranco*, turn left onto the stone-paved *camino* to climb above the main track road which leads along the next mountain ridge where the settlement of **El Joradillo**, 140 m is clinging. Arriving here, immediately cross over the road (asphalt at this point) and then cross over the plateau to pass a house. The *camino* continues through terraces and then descends into the next ra-

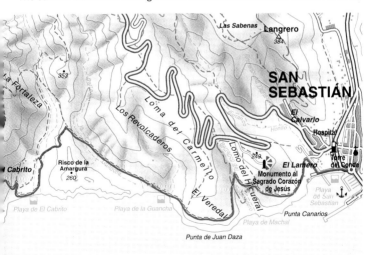

vine: the Barranco de Chinguarime. After a quarter hour reach the valley floor to meet the track road again; here left, only to finally leave it behind just after passing the plantation. Cross over the *barranco* floor to the right and ascend the opposite slope along a lovely, old *camino*, passing beautifully-formed boulder blocks, to reach the next mountain ridge (a good 20 min). At first, the trail ascends for a short distance along the left edge of the crest then leads bearing right through barren, overgrown terraces, only a few minutes later to ascend in a direct line along the mountain ridge. At the same time, pass immediately to the left of an old stone house then 10 min afterwards between another two old houses. Just after, pass yet another house perched on the right-hand edge of the mountain ridge. Continue ascending along the edge of the crest for a few minutes until the *camino* bears right through the more-or-less gully-like Barranco de la Vasa and then forks: immediately to the right you can reach some ruined houses with a threshing yard, but we take the fork to the left to ascend at first along the right-hand edge of the *barranco* gully. Passing the ruins of houses and a cement cistern, soon pass another abandoned settlement to the right. The *camino* returns again, now bearing left along the edge of the *barranco* gully, only to turn away again a few minutes later to the right, to begin an ascent passing two palm trees, along a craggy ridge to the **Casas de Contrera**, 400 m, a small, abandoned settlement with a prominent two-story house that (still) boasts a wooden balcony.

The trail forks below the two-story house: to the left along the ridgeline, a continued ascent to the trail connecting Seima and Jerduñe (→Walk 5) is possible. Our continued route toward San Sebastián, however, forks to the right. This descends immediately, sometimes over rock and very indistinct, into the Barranco de Contrera. Descend along the *barranco* floor for about 50 m then the *camino* ascends on the opposite side. About 10 min from Contrera, pass a solitary house then cross over the gentle valley notch of the Barranco del Guincho to continue an ascent bearing right over the plateau which follows. About a half hour from Contrera, perched on the next mountain ridge before us, we can already spot **Seima**, 530 m, which we reach in another 20 min by ascending along the valley floor of the Cañada Sabina Redonda.

In the tiny, abandoned settlement meet up with an intersecting cobblestone trail (→Walk 5), follow this to the right along the gentle ridgeline towards the sea. After a quarter hour, a small trail forks to the left to descend into the Barranco Juan de Vera. However, we remain steadfast along the ridge and about 20 min later, near a power pylon, return to the ridgeline to already catch a view below of the Playa de El Cabrito with the holiday resort of the same name surrounded by verdant garden grounds. Continue for a short stretch descending along the ridgeline then the well-maintained cobblestone trail bears to the left to descend steeply to El Cabrito. Arriving at the

Seima – grain was cultivated here in the past – nowadays, the hamlet is abandoned.

first houses, the trail merges into an intersecting trail. Along this to the right reach the nearby **Playa de El Cabrito**.

After a good, long break begin the final stretch. At first follow the road that leads along the beach, then pass the wall enclosing the holiday resort and continue into the Barranco Juan de Vera. After some minutes, cross over the *barranco* floor and directly below the power pylon climb in zigzags along a *camino*. After a steep ascent lasting about 10 min, a traverse follows to the left reaching a small saddle on the crest of the mountain ridge, 147 m (the trail forks here); take the right fork onto a steep, somewhat exposed *camino* descending into the Barranco de la Guancha, where the trail leads along the opposite valley flank to reach the nearby **Playa de la Guancha**. At the end of the beach is a solitary white house.

Pass the house then enter a *barranco* gully to ascend along this, bearing right onto the next mountain ridge. Now a steady traverse begins, remaining above the coast. Soon cross over a road and the Barranco del Revolcadero, then finally reach a crucifix (a good ¾ hr from Playa de la Guancha). From here enjoy a marvellous view of the island's capital lying before us. Now the *camino* descends bearing to the left and, in the industrial area behind the harbour bay, meets a street that leads to the right ending at the seaside promenade of **San Sebastián**. The bus stop is located on the main road in the village centre.

12 From Santiago to Lo del Gato

Circuit route through picturesque villages and lush gardens near Santiago

(Playa de Santiago –) Taco – Pastrana – Lo del Gato – El Cabezo – Taco

Location: Playa de Santiago, 10 m.
Starting point: Taco, 200 m, on the main road from Santiago to Pastrana / Guarimiar, about 3 km from the junction of the access road in Laguna de Santiago (no bus service; ¾ hr by foot from Laguna de Santiago – bus stop for lines 2, 5).
Walking time: Taco – Pastrana 20 min, Pastrana – Lo del Gato 40 min, Lo del Gato – Taco 1¾ hrs; total time 2¾ hrs.
Ascent: 500 m (from Santiago add another 200 m).
Grade: The ascent to Lo del Gato is easy. The continued route to El Cabezo is narrow and precipitous, requiring sure-footedness and an excellent head for heights.
Refreshment: Only in Santiago.
Combination possible with Walks 6, 7 and 9.

This little »orientation walk« in the mountains above Santiago is more than it seems: while the ascent from Taco to Lo del Gato can be easily undertaken by just about anybody, the steep, sometimes narrow and precipitous stretch to El Cabezo requires absolute sure-footedness and also from time-to-time a bit of path-finding talent. Therefore, the less-experienced walker is recommended to return from Lo del Gato via the more popular route – but even without an »alpine touch«, this is a very lovely short walk!

From the fork in the road in the hamlet of **Taco**, ascend to the right along the road towards Pastrana enjoying a lovely view of El Rumbazo and El Cabezo. After a quarter hour reach the idyllically-situated village of **Pastrana**, 250 m, to follow the village street straight to its end and a turn-about. Here, left of the street, a wide *camino* continues straight on. This leads somewhat above the Barranco de Benchijigua and passes through lush terraces of banana, medlar, orange, date and fig trees as well as vine-yards and potato patches. Passing a last house, descend to the floor of the *barranco* to ascend along this for a good 200 m (100 m on – a *gofio* mill to the left) until the broad *camino* again turns away to the right. Pass above two round water reservoirs then continue ascending into the valley. Before us, the mighty Roque de Agando begins to appear little-by-little and, after the valley takes a hook, we can already see the houses of Lo del Gato. Remain on the broad trail traversing the slope until this forks just before the village (about ½ hr from Pastrana). The trail to the right continues ascending towards Benchijigua (→Walk 6), but we take the left trail crossing the *barranco* and ascending steeply through terraces, bearing right at the fork in front of the first house (after this, bear left) to reach the end of the street in **Lo del Gato**, 420 m.

Now follow the *camino* continuing on from the end of the street in a southerly direction through the village (always following the street lamps). Above the last house and below a small water reservoir, the trail swings to the right into a side valley (along a covered water channel) immediately passing another small water reservoir. Do not change over with the distinct trail to the left side of the valley, instead continue ascending along the valley floor for about 30 m to finally climb to the left on a stony *camino* (cairn). The old trail begins as a well-maintained one, but starting at a large cave (to the right away from the trail) suffers from slide damage and debris. Nevertheless, orientation is no problem – the trail continues a steep ascent bearing slightly to the left sometimes over rock. After half an hour reach the edge of a slope. From here continue left almost on the level to cross to the next slope's crest and then to the right on the back side of the ridge to continue traversing the slope (passing between a palm tree to the left and a small, dark cliff face to the right, about 300 m below a dilapidated house). The main trail leads always diagonally, traversing the slope through overgrown terraces then crosses over a gully and continues an ascent bearing left to a small plateau above a cliff. After a pleasant 5-min traverse of the slope, the trail ascends as a narrow, somewhat precipitous footpath for a short stretch towards the foot of a long, extended cliff face and there meets a broad intersecting trail descending from El Azadoe. Turn left here. The trail traverses the hang with exposed stretches and after a good 10 min, interrupted by two descending bends (before these and to the left – a lovely plateau to rest and enjoy views), only to change over 10 min later to the right side of the ridge (ignore a left fork). With the road to Guarimiar in view, descend to the right – to our right we soon see the hamlet of Guarimiar with its chapel – and continue later by bearing left along the slope above the road. After a good quarter hour, pass by a small waterworks then immediately after reach a road in the hamlet **El Cabezo**, 250 m, that descends to the right to the valley road. Along this to the left, steadily descending into the valley to return to **Taco** (10 min).

The Western Island

Valle Gran Rey and surroundings

In the south-west, Gomera unfolds its very special charms: gentle valleys with palm groves and ingeniously constructed terraces, quaint villages and untamed *barrancos* are typical for this region which boasts one of the most enchanting landscapes of the Canary Archipelago.

Especially noteworthy is the majestic **Valle Gran Rey** (Valley of the Great King) incised into the landscape in canyon-like grandeur. Enclosed by plunging cliffs up to 800 m high, a singular agricultural terrain has been developed here, not to be compared to any other on the Canary Islands. The long, drawn-out Barranco del Valle Gran Rey, thanks to its location and lovely beaches at the ocean estuary, has attracted travellers for a very long time. Once an insider tip among hippies and societal drop-outs in the 60's, the area has been taken over step-by-step by the tourist trade, remoulding it into the island's tourist centre. Fortunately the valley and its villages – especially La Calera – have managed to retain their unique flair.

In the environs of Valle Gran Rey, holiday-makers will find a superbly developed walking realm, making many walks possible to begin without the need for transportation. Popular excursion spots and starting points for walks are offered by the picturesque mountain villages above the Valle Gran Rey, perched in a row along the borders of the national park. Especially attractive

A bird's-eye view of La Calera and La Playa – from the Las Pilas plateau.

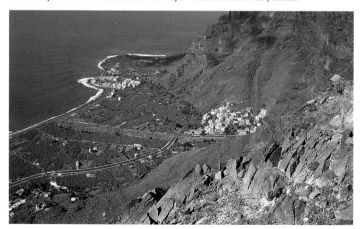

The lovely beach of La Playa.

is a start from the hamlet Chipude, one of the oldest settlements on the island, to reach the commanding table-top mountain Fortaleza, 1243 m, and to one of Gomera's most savage gorges – the Barranco de Erque. El Cercado, the island's pottery-producing village and Las Hayas are ideal for an excursion into the national park. This is also true of Arure, additionally offering ventures along superb walking routes to the west coast, through the Taguluche and Alojera Valleys.

STARTING POINTS FOR WALKS

Chipude, 1080 m / El Cercado, 1030 m / Las Hayas, 1000 m

Beautifully situated villages above the Valle Gran Rey on the Arure – Carretera del Sur road (bus stops for the lines 1, 6 and 7). Ideal starting points for walks into the Valle Gran Rey, to the Fortaleza, in the Parque Nacional de Garajonay and to Arure.

Arure, 826 m

Village on the main road to Valle Gran Rey (bus stop for bus lines 1 and 6). Walking trails to Las Hayas, Valle Gran Rey, Taguluche, Alojera and in the Parque Nacional de Garajonay.

Valle Gran Rey, 0 – 500 m

The »Valley of the Great King« is an eldorado for walkers and is highly recommended for a Gomera holiday sojourn (bus lines 1 and 6). Walking trails to the mountain villages above the Valle Gran Rey, along the neighbouring mountain ranges and through the Barranco de Argaga as well as the Barranco de Arure.

Taguluche, 200 m / Alojera, 200 m

The island's western villages, accessible via a road from Chorros de Epina (bus stop for line 4). Walking trails to Valle Gran Rey, Arure, Chorros de Epina and Arguamul.

13 Fortaleza, 1243 m

Short walk with a bit of a scramble on a mysterious table-top mountain

Chipude – Apartadero – Pavón – Fortaleza (– Garajonay) and back

Starting point: The church square of Chipude, 1080 m (bus stop for lines 1, 6, 7).
Walking time: Chipude – Fortaleza Saddle ½ hr, Fortaleza Saddle – Fortaleza ½ hr, return ¾ hr; total time 1¾ hrs.
Ascent: not quite 200 m.
Grade: The ascent requires a bit of scrambling (I) at the end, otherwise an easy, short walk. It is best to postpone the ascent to the peak after rainfall or when foggy.
Refreshment: In Chipude and in Apartadero / Pavón bar/restaurants.
Alternatives: Ascent to Garajonay: from the Fortaleza Saddle take the cobblestone trail ascending in a north-easterly direction until merging into a track road (10 min), continue the ascent along this to the main road nearby, then right along this to reach a forester's house (10 min). Here turn left on the Camino forestal Las Tajoras. After

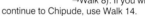

5 min a road merges from the left; here continue straight on. Also at the next fork continue straight on passing through a barrier. Immediately after and just before the lovely Argumame pine forest (10 min from the forester's house), turn right onto a forestry trail (sign »Alto de Garajonay«) ascending straight on for a half hour until merging onto a track (chain barrier). Turn right onto the track then soon after to the left to climb to the peak of Garajonay, 1487 m (1¼ hrs from the Fortaleza Saddle). From here a descent possible to Laguna Grande (→Walk 44) or to the road junction at Pajarito (bus stop for line 1; →Walk 8). If you wish to continue to Chipude, use Walk 14.
Combination possible with Walks 14, 15, 16 and 20.
Tip: The walk can also begin in Pavón on the road to La Dama (40 min shorter).

Dropping steeply from all sides, the Fortaleza de Chipude not only counts as one of the island's most panoramic overlooks, but was also once an important ritual site for the native inhabitants – a magical place, especially when wisps of fog swirl and whirl over the plateau!
From the church square in **Chipude**, follow the main road for 100 m towards San Sebastián then turn left onto a broad cobblestone trail. This ascends shortly, crosses over the main road again and then descends to the road towards La Dama, following this for only 20 m before leaving it by bearing left and ascending. With a view of the Fortaleza, the *camino* leads only for a few minutes above the road before reaching the settlement of **Apartadero** and then merging once again into it. Passing the Los Camioneros bar and after a sharp right-hand bend reach **Pavón**, 1100 m.

The flat crest of Fortaleza's peak faces a sheer drop into the Erque Gorge.

20 m after the transformer tower, a cobblestone street ascends to the left away from the road and then ends in front of a gentle valley notch. Passing a house built of natural stone, ascend to the right of the valley. Near the last houses, you can see an old winepress (to the left of the trail). Shortly after, reach the **Fortaleza Saddle**, 1120 m, to meet up with an intersecting cobblestone trail next to a stone house (this leads to the left towards Garajonay). However, follow the trail for a few metres to the right then fork left onto a steep, ascending footpath bearing slightly to the left close to the ridgeline and leading to the foot of the Fortaleza cliff wall. Now the prettiest stretch of the ascent begins: via a step-like rock climb with stretches of easy but adrenaline-activating scrambling (I), climb to a small, craggy secondary peak. From here to the right over boulders reach the drawn-out crest of the **Fortaleza**. Be sure to ramble a bit along the plateau – especially impressive are the overlooks from the southern edge, with a downward view into the savage Barranco de Erque and views of the south coast and La Dama below. Bravehearts may wish to attempt a foray along the extremely narrow and precipitous sometimes knife-edged southern ridge.

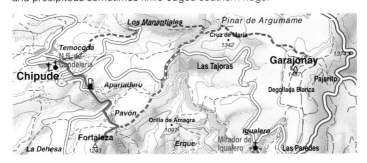

14 From Chipude to Garajonay, 1487 m

Pleasant high ramble to the highest point of the island

Chipude – Pavón – Fortaleza Saddle (– Fortaleza) – Igualero – Garajonay – Los Manantiales – Chipude

Starting point: The church square of Chipude, 1080 m (bus stop for lines 1, 6 and 7).

Walking time: Chipude – Fortaleza Saddle ½ hr, Fortaleza Saddle – high mountain trail fork 20 min, high mountain trail to Igualero (main road) 1¼ hrs, Igualero – Garajonay a good ½ hr, Garajonay – Los Manantiales not quite 1 hr, Los Manantiales – Chipude 25 min; total time 4¼ hrs.

Ascent: About 450 m.

Grade: Essentially easy, mostly pleasant walk on distinct trails.

Refreshment: In Chipude and in Apartadero / Pavón bar/restaurants.

Alternatives: Ascent to the Fortaleza from the Fortaleza Saddle (¾ hr there and back, →Walk 13). Descent from Garajonay to the road junction at Pajarito (→Walk 8; bus stop for line 1).

Combination possible with Walks 8, 13, 15, 16 and 44.

Garajonay is not only the most visited but also the most approachable walking destination on Gomera, but most walkers prefer tackling this peak via the shorter ascents from Laguna Grande, Contadero or Pajarito. This route is much more peaceful and inspiring, leading along a pleasant, particularly panoramic high mountain trail to Igualero, Gomera's highest village, then climbing from there to the crest of Garajonay. If this peak isn't enough for you, there is another popular one to »take« – the Fortaleza.

From the church square of **Chipude** follow the main road towards San Sebastián then 150 m on, turn left onto the broad cobblestone trail that ascends for a short stretch to cross over the main road and on the other side descends to the road to La Dama. After 20 m, a camino forking left continues on parallel to the road and leads to the hamlet of **Apartadero** then

Backwards view to Fortaleza from the high trail.

merges with the road again. Past the Los Camioneros bar and after a sharp right-hand bend reach the hamlet **Pavón**. 20 m after the transformer tower on the side of the road, a cobblestone street ascends to the left and ends just before a small gentle valley notch. Here right through the notch climbing to the **Fortaleza Saddle**, 1120 m, to reach an intersecting cobblestone trail (to the right a possible excursion onto the Fortaleza, →Walk 13).

Just before reaching Igualero.

Continue the route by turning left onto the cobblestone trail and after 10 min meet the track road to Erque. Descend to the right along this for about 10 min until crossing a *barranco* in a sharp right-hand bend. Here, immediately after the bend, a sign-posted *camino* to Igualero turns left. This ascends in a pleasant, gentle high mountain walk below the timberline traversing the slope and opening a fantastic view of the Fortaleza. Near a high tension power pylon catch a downwards view of the hamlet Erque nestled in the chasm-like *barranco* of the same name. After a good 20 min cross a small stream bed then shortly after pass a second power pylon. In easy up-and-down walking with a lovely view of La Dama and the neighbouring islands of El Hierro and La Palma, traverse the slope towards these. Only after passing the third power pylon (10 min) does the trail become somewhat steeper. Now at about the same altitude as the Fortaleza peak, this disappears from view after a left-hand bend (here left at a fork). Our *camino* now climbs through overgrown terraces to the first houses of **Igualero**, 1300 m (about 1 hr after forking from the track). After passing the first houses, the main trail hooks away to the left to merge into a cobblestone street leading to the main road (10 min; bus stop shelter for lines 1 and 6).

Follow the main road 10 m to the right then turn left onto a footpath passing to the right of a waterworks. 10 m after passing the waterworks cross the little *barranco* gully to the left. Immediately after, the sometimes stone-paved path ascends parallel to the gully with a water conduit running alongside, heading in a fairly straight line through the pine forest. After a steep 10-min climb, pass a stone house. Immediately after meet a track road and turn left (cater-corner to the right a possible ascent along a path via the antennae-crowned secondary peak to Garajonay). After a few minutes, a forestry road merges from the left into our track road then a quarter hour later another forestry road coming from Chipude merges sharply from the left (the return route later on). A good 100 m later reach another track forking off (chained) – continue to the right here (the track forking left leads to the mountain road with the car park Alto del Contadero). A few minutes later bear left at the fork

On the return route, we pass the hamlet of Los Manantiales.

to climb to the overlook platform at **Garajonay**, 1487 m; when weather permits enjoy a wonderful 360° panoramic view.

Return along the forestry track bearing right at the fork near the peak then soon left at the next fork passing the chain barrier onto the track towards Chipude (sign). A good 100 m on, reach yet another fork – here right, descending on the steep road (sign »Chipude – Laguna Grande«), while enjoying a fabulous view of the Fortaleza. After about 20 min reach a major fork (right to the pretty pine forest Pinar de Argumame, sign), and bear left here. At the next junction (another chain barrier) a forestry road forks hard to the right; but we continue by bearing only a bit to the right onto a signposted trail enclosed by steep sides. This becomes a regular road in a few minutes then shortly after swings to the left and forks – bear right to descend. Soon the road becomes a stepped *camino* passing vineyards and descending to the end of a track road in the hamlet of **Los Manantiales**, 1100 m. Here right to continue via the *camino* and, at the first house, left with a red arrow marking to descend to an intersecting trail. Continue left along this until, in front of a house, a broad intersecting trail leads to the right descending to the valley floor. On the other flank of the valley, a gently ascending trail continues, bearing right along the slope, and forks 5 min later. Here left to the ridgeline then descend through a small valley and continue along a cobblestone street down to the church square of **Chipude**.

15 From Chipude to Erque

Steep descent through the dramatic, untamed and unspoilt Barranco de Erque

Chipude – Fortaleza Saddle (– Fortaleza) – Erque (– Erquito) – Chipude

Starting point: The church square of Chipude, 1080 m (bus stop for lines 1, 6 and 7).

Walking time: Chipude – Fortaleza Saddle ½ hr, Fortaleza Saddle – Mirador de Erque 1 hr, Mirador de Erque – Chipude 1½ hrs; total time 3 hrs (Alternative to Erquito add 1 hr).

Ascent: About 500 m.

Grade: A steep descent from the Fortaleza Saddle requiring sure-footedness and an excellent head for heights; some stretches over rock (easy scrambling, l) but hardly precipitous. Ascent from Erque to the track road along an overgrown sometimes slide-damaged *camino*.

Refreshment: Bar/restaurants in Chipude and in Apartadero / Pavón.

Alternative: From Erque to Erquito: At the first houses of Erque do not turn left but continue straight on along the main trail descending lightly. After a few minutes reach a rocky spine with two prominent rock needles somewhat below (on the other side of the valley the continuing trail to Erquito can be clearly seen). Crossing the rocky spine at about its middle, descend lightly on the trail bearing left which leads onto terraces (somewhat overgrown) and here 50 m on, descend to the right into the stream bed of the Barranco de Erque. Bearing right, leave the stream bed and immediately ascend left for about 20 m to the beginning of the narrow *camino* to Erquito, climbing out of the valley and traversing the slope. This is somewhat overgrown and after a few minutes crosses a scree-filled gully, soon after passing a mountain spur crowned with a power pylon. After ½ hr reach the crest of a ridge to catch a view of Erquito's scattered houses. Now descend along the rocky trail bearing left into the valley following the pylons. Shortly before the palm tree grove turn left crossing a small bridge to reach the first houses of Erquito, 700 m, an almost completely abandoned village (a good ¾ hr from Erque). The trail continues always straight on without losing altitude, passing through the village directly to the right of a house and telegraph poles (do not descend to the right; the village chapel is above to the left), soon merging into a road which forks immediately after crossing a *barranco*. Here take a sharp left onto a cobblestone trail ascending and passing more houses. Below the last, white house to the left of the main trail turn left onto a trail that is at first hard to see but is then distinct (straight on to continue to La Dama, about 3½ hrs). The trail returns immediately back into the small *barranco* ascending steeply on the other side along the slope. A few minutes later at the fork continue straight (left) to reach the track road leading from Erquito's village chapel to Erque. About ½ hr later a track forks left to Mirador de Erque, here right onto the track to continue the ascent. A good 15 min later, immediately in front of the breach in the cliff, the trail coming from Erque merges from the left into the track road.

Combination possible with Walks 13, 14 and 16.

Maybe there are walking trails on Gomera much prettier than this steep, rocky route through the charming hamlet of Erque, surrounded by palm tree groves and cultivated terraces – but this only highlights the grandeur of the setting: the gorge-like Barranco de Erque and the mighty, majestic Fortaleza dominating the scene; also, scrambling fans will surely be delighted while climbing here and perhaps, before or after completing the »Erque circuit«, may wish to try their luck at tackling the Fortaleza itself.

From the church square in **Chipude** follow the main road towards San Sebastián and 100 m on turn left onto the broad cobblestone trail that after a short ascent crosses the main road and descends on the other side to the road towards La Dama. 20 m on, the *camino* continues cater-corner left reaching the hamlet **Apartadero** then merges again with the road. Past the Los Camioneros bar, and after a sharp right-hand bend reach the hamlet **Pavón**. 20 m after the transformer tower on the side of the road, a cobblestone street ascends to the left ending before a gentle valley notch. Here right into the valley notch climbing to the **Fortaleza Saddle**, 1120 m, and a few metres past a stone house reach an intersecting cobblestone trail (to the right, a possible detour to climb the Fortaleza, →Walk 13).

Here take a sharp right following the cobblestone trail towards the Fortaleza for about 20 m then bear left at the nature reserve sign to continue over the saddle towards the Fortaleza. On the other side of the ridgeline, more

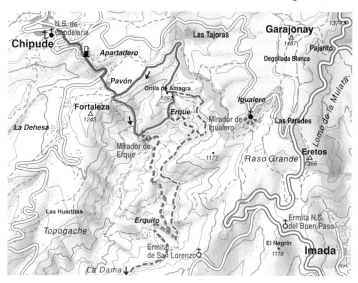

From the Fortaleza Saddle, an excursion can be made to the table-top mountain.

houses appear. Our *camino* now descends lightly bearing right and passes between the two highest houses then leads into the abyss of the *barranco* at the foot of the Fortaleza. After a good 10-min steep descent through a cactus wilderness, a small path forks to the left; however we continue to the right over a short, narrow outcrop then descend to the left over steps along a small, somewhat risky and precipitous cliff wall. Now a traverse of 50 m to the left, then again bearing left crossing rock and steps descending to a small mountain ridge; here between two *barranco* gullies continue the steep descent into the valley – the narrow path is sometimes difficult to discern. About a half hour from the Fortaleza Saddle, already past a few palm trees, descend another stretch of beguiling light scramble along a small cliff face. The trail is now more scree-slippery underfoot and after another quarter hour reaches the floor of the *barranco* (it is best to descend to the *barranco* floor by bearing left). On the opposite side, a lovely *camino* continues the descent into the valley and forks 100 m on – here continue right descending lightly. Now begin a traverse passing below a mighty, colossal crag shimmering in a multitude of colours. Afterward, the first houses of Erque appear ahead. A couple of short scrambling passages demand our attention, then we reach the houses.

The main trail continues straight on descending lightly. However, before the first houses, we turn to the left and ascend over a small ridge then over steps to the **Mirador de Erque**, 800 m, where the track road to Erque ends – a lovely rest area with a splendid view of the Barranco de Erque and the Fortaleza. Follow the road into the valley. A good 5 min later, before a sharp right-hand bend with palm trees and about 20 m before a house, ascend left onto a somewhat overgrown *camino*, at first very difficult to make out. After a good 10 min pass directly to the left of an old house. There follows a short, somewhat confusing stretch, then the old stone paving can be discerned from time to time. In a steady, steep ascent via an extremely overgrown stony trail finally reach the track road ascending from Erque and Erquito (¾ hr from the *mirador*). On the other side of this, an extremely overgrown *camino* continues, but we follow the pleasant track to the left through the breach in the cliff. 10 min later cross over a *barranco* (before the sharp left-hand bend, a trail forks sharply to the right towards Igualero, →Walk 14). A good 10 min later in a sharp right-hand bend, a cobblestone trail forks off to the left and reaches the **Fortaleza Saddle** in not quite 10 min. From here via the approach route return to **Chipude**.

The romantic palm village Erque; in the background – the Fortaleza.

16 From Chipude to Valle Gran Rey

Gratifying walk »à la Gomera«

Chipude – La Matanza (– Ermita N.S. de Guadalupe) – Ermita de los Reyes – La Calera

Starting point: The church square of Chipude, 1080 m (bus stop for lines 1, 6, 7).
Destination: La Calera, 50 m, in the Valle Gran Rey (bus stop for lines 1, 6).
Walking time: Chipude – La Matanza ¾ hr, La Matanza – the fork on the crest of the ridge above the Valle Gran Rey ¾ hr, ridge crest – Ermita de los Reyes 1 hr, Ermita de los Reyes – La Calera ½ hr; total time 3 hrs (return to Chipude 3½ hrs).
Descent: 1100 m with short stretches of ascent.
Grade: Essentially easy descent route,

nevertheless requiring sure-footedness due to steep stony stretches along *caminos*.
Refreshment: In Chipude and in La Calera bar/restaurants.
Alternative: If you prefer a circuit walk, you can use Walk 25 from La Matanza ascending to El Cercado (1 hr), from there via Walk 20 return to Chipude (½ hr).
Combination possible with Walks 13–15, 17, 20, 23–27.
Tip: Excellent beaches in La Playa – bring along your swimming gear!

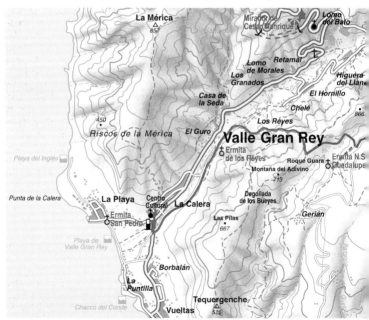

The mountain village Chipude; in the background – the Fortaleza.

This descent route imparts lasting impressions of Gomera's landscapes: passing the romantic La Matanza pasturage, the trail leads through the Barranco de Argaga (still quite tame at this point – sporting fig cactus and palm trees) then continues to the mountain ridge above the Valle Gran Rey. From here a stony but pardonably, panoramic cobblestone trail dips down to the Ermita de los Reyes and continues to La Calera – now only a stone's-throw to the lovely Playa de Valle Gran Rey where you can unpack your swimming gear and end the day in rest and relaxation. Now that's a gratifying walk »à la Gomera«!

Across from the church square of **Chipude**, to the right of the La Candelaria bar, descend along the cobblestone street and after a few minutes merge with the main road to El Cercado. Follow this 20 m to the left then turn right onto a road that immediately forks – here right following the lanterns. Past the last houses, an old *camino* continues leading pleasantly into the valley and crossing a road right away. Always straight on, follow the increasingly stony trail along the slope (do not fork right into the Barranco de los Manantiales). After half an hour reach a fork – here a sharp right to continue along the broad *camino* that bears left into the valley. On the floor of the valley next to the **La Matanza** pasturage, 780 m, meet the main trail descending from El Cercado.

Straight on along the sheer cliff edge of the Valle Gran Rey, an extremely precipitously-constructed cliff trail, closed due to rock slide damage, continues towards La Vizcaína – already a few metres along, this opens a stupendous view over the beautiful valley (a pretty spot for a break). However, we follow the main trail to the left, passing a solitary palm tree. The distinct path leads along the left-hand slope of the Barranco de Argaga (which begins near La Matanza) always following along or near an abandoned water channel. After 10 min pass below a property with vineyards. 15 min later a distinct *camino* crosses our channel trail. Take a sharp right onto this and descend (cairns; straight on the channel trail a detour is possible to the little **Ermita de Nuestra Señora de Guadalupe**, 750 m, perched on the mountain spur Roque de Gurara; 20 min there and back). After 10 min the cobblestone trail crosses over the Barranco de Argaga and continues straight ahead on the other side bearing left in an easy ascent to reach the crest of the ridge above the Valle Gran Rey. The trail forks at this point (left along the ridgeline continues a route towards Tequergenche →Walk 26). We turn right onto the cobblestone trail leading towards the valley and opening superb views of the middle Valle Gran Rey. Always following the stony *camino* which is sometimes unpleasantly scree-slippery underfoot (soon leading to, then along, a mountain ridge towards the valley) after not quite 1 hr, below one of the first houses, meet up with a broad intersecting trail – here left to reach **Ermita de los Reyes**, 150 m, in a good 5 min.

If you prefer not to continue on to La Calera, descend the steps at the end of the church square, cross over the road at the *barranco* floor and then the stream bed with rushes and reeds and on the other side climb to the main road in El Guro (a good 5 min, bus stop for lines 1 and 6). But, we descend only a few steps then follow the small trail continuing straight on which merges into a road after a few minutes. Continue along this towards the valley until reaching the road bridge in **La Calera** – 50 m before the bridge, steps ascend to the right to the main road. To continue on to the beach, ascend shortly along the main road then take a sharp left turn onto the little street leading to **La Playa** (¼ hr).

Crossing the wild and idyllic Barranco de Argaya.

17 From El Cercado to Valle Gran Rey

Pleasant, panoramic descent route into the »Valley of the Great King«

El Cercado – La Vizcaína – Lomo del Balo/La Calera (– Ermita de los Reyes – La Matanza – El Cercado)

Starting point: El Cercado, 1030 m (bus stop for lines 1, 6, 7).
Destination: La Vizcaína, 420 m (nearest bus stop for lines 1 and 6 in Lomo del Balo, 430 m), or La Calera, 50 m (bus stop for lines 1, 6).
Walking time: El Cercado – La Vizcaína not quite 1½ hrs, continued route to Lomo del Balo ¼ hr, via the Ermita de los Reyes to La Calera 1¼ hrs; total time 1¾ hrs (Lomo del Balo) respectively 2¾ hrs (La Calera).
Descent: 1000 m.
Grade: Partially pleasant, partially steep descent route via good cobblestone trails

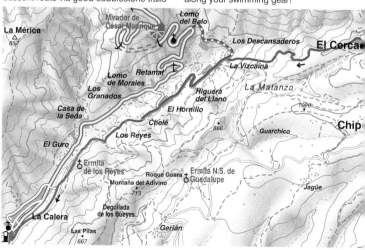

(sure-footedness required), from La Vizcaína sometimes via roads and tracks.
Refreshment: In El Cercado, Lomo del Balo and La Calera bar/restaurants.

Alternative: If you wish to turn back to El Cercado, we recommend using Walk 25. A good 5 min before the Ermita de los Reyes this forks away to the left (total time for the circuit route El Cercado – La Vizcaína – Los Reyes – La Matanza – El Cercado not quite 5 hrs).

Combination possible with Walks 16 and 20.

Tip: Excellent beaches in La Playa – bring along your swimming gear!

El Cercado is renowned for pottery.

This is perhaps the most beautiful descent route into the Valle Gran Rey, revealing all the charms offered by the »Valley of the Great King«: the walk passes along the chasm-like Barranco del Agua, opening remarkable views over the carefully-constructed terraced slopes of the valley where our descent will soon follow towards La Calera. Due to the popularity of the route, we have also included it in Walk 23 but in the opposite direction.

Directly across from the bar »Maria« at the village limits towards Las Hayas, a road forks away from the main road in **El Cercado**. This passes a few houses and descends along the edge of the water-blessed, steep-walled Barranco del Agua. After 5 min reach a depression to enjoy a lovely view including El Cercado as well as Chipude with the Fortaleza. Here turn right onto the broad *camino*, at first leading on the level along the slope then pleasantly descending – somewhat steeper stretches only occurring from time to time. After not quite a half hour reach a short stretch which sweeps to the right then, a bit later, skirt around a cliff face by bearing slightly to the right. Enjoying a fantastic view of the Valle Gran Rey descend again through a small valley basin. After a total of not quite 1 hr, reach a steep *barranco* gully then cross it. About 50 m on, a distinct *camino* forks left (marked with red dots) – this extremely steeply-constructed, precipitous cliff route climbs in 20 min to the La Matanza pasturage, but is closed at the upper section due to rock slide damage. We remain on the main trail continuing straight ahead. This descends steeply again for a short stretch but soon levels out after passing another gully. Begin to pass the first terraces of La Vizcaína then a quarter hour after the fork for the cliff route, pass to the right of a wa-

View from Lomo del Balo to the steep cliff wall above the Barranco del Agua – the route leads through this.

terworks. Now it is only a 10-min descent to reach the street in **La Vizcaína**, 420 m – a wonderful stretch passing palm trees, cultivated terraces and quaint village houses.

Turning right on the street, reach the main road in **Lomo del Balo** in a quarter hour (bus stop for lines 1 and 6). However, it is lovelier to continue the descent through the Valle Gran Rey. During the pleasant stretch along the street in peace and quiet, savour this marvellous pastoral scene with pretty houses and idyllic gardens. The street descends in a bend to the right then forks in El Hornillo (to the right through the *barranco* cross over to the main road on the other side of the valley). We continue the route by turning left on the street; this comes to an end a few minutes later in Chelé, in front of a dark, fantastic cliff riddled with holes. Here continue right on a *camino* that leads along the foot of this curious work of Nature where numerous caves have been made into stalls. Not quite 10 min later, a trail forks left to the La Matanza pasturage; a good 5 min on, reach the **Ermita de los Reyes**, 150 m.

If you prefer not to continue on to La Calera, descend the steps at the end of the church square, cross over the road at the *barranco* floor and then the stream bed with rushes and reeds and on the other side climb to the main road in El Guro (a good 5 min, bus stop for lines 1 and 6). But, we descend only a few steps then follow the small trail continuing straight on which merges into a road after a few minutes. Continue along this towards the valley until reaching the road bridge in **La Calera** – 50 m before the bridge, steps ascend to the right to the main road. To continue on to the beach, ascend shortly along the main road then take a sharp left turn onto the little street leading to **La Playa** (¼ hr).

The seaside promenade of La Playa; in the background – La Calera.

18 From Las Hayas to Jardín de Las Creces

Short, pleasant circuit route through the Cedro primeval forest

Las Hayas – Jardín de Las Creces – Las Hayas

Starting point: Bar/restaurant »La Montaña« (Casa Efigenia) in Las Hayas, 1000 m (bus stop for lines 1, 6, 7).
Walking time: Las Hayas – Jardín de Las

Creces 40 min, Jardín de Las Creces – Las Hayas ¾ hr; total time 1½ hrs.
Ascent: About 150 m.
Grade: Easy, hardly strenuous forest route through the Parque Nacional de Garajonay, somewhat slippery when wet.
Refreshment: In Las Hayas bar/restaurants.
Combination possible with Walks 19–22.
Tip: The route can also begin on the Carretera del Centro near the fork of the forestry road to Jardín de Las Creces (sign; between the road junction at Apartacaminos, about 2.3 km away and the road junction Cruce de Las Hayas, about 1 km away). From here, 5 min by foot to the little picnic place Jardín de Las Creces.

This lovely circuit walk through the national park established by the national park administration bestows a multitude of botanical treats – a first-rate exploratory route for anyone wanting to acquaint himself to this region of pristine, almost primeval laurel forest.

Begin the route near one of the island's most original restaurants – nestled in the shade of towering eucalyptus trees – Casa Efigenia (bar/restaurant »La Montaña«) in **Las Hayas**. Just above the Casa Efigenia, in the next bend in the main road, a street forks off to the left and then ends. Passing to the left of a house, a trail continues – ascend along this always straight on. After 5 min pass to the left of the church then immediately after, pass a cistern. Now the trail becomes a path leading straight on, bearing left and entering a scrub wood (50 m on – a national park sign). 35 m after the national park sign bear right at the fork. The path leads pretty much on the level through the lovely forest and after a good 5 min merges into a broad forestry trail (signs »Carretera dorsal / Las Hayas«); turn right here. A good 20 min later reach a small picnic place surrounded by the lovely laurel forest – **Jardín de Las Creces**, 1040 m – a number of picnic tables offer an opportunity for a break; a tap provides fresh spring water for your canteen.

The broad forestry trail continues straight on to reach the high road in 5 min. However, at the picnic place next to the national park sign (sign »Las Creces«) we turn left onto the narrow *camino* descending at first on the right flank, after 10 min along the left flank of a gentle valley notch – a delightful nature trail passing ferns up to 6 feet tall, towering laurel trees, hanging creepers and patches of moss and lichen. Not quite 20 min from Las Creces, the trail forks: the left fork returns back to the approach route (after not quite 15 min, at the end ascending steeply, the path merges into the forestry trail at the signs »Carretera dorsal / Las Hayas«). We continue straight on along the gentle valley notch and now change back over to the right flank. A few minutes later where a valley merges from the left, the forest begins to thin out. The landscape changes abruptly: ferns and laurel trees have disappeared making way for an encroaching scrub wood. Shortly after, meet a forestry track and ascend along this to the left (to the right – a descent to Arure, ½ hr). 5 min later bear left at a fork then after another few minutes **Las Hayas** appears before us. The broad, washed-out forestry trail leads straight on to the village, at the end passing corrals, then merges into the main road, with the bar/restaurant »La Montaña« to the left.

The little picnic area »Jardín de las Creces« is located at the turnaround point of the walk.

19 **From Arure to Raso de la Bruma**

From terraced pastoral land into the primeval forest

Arure – Cañada de Jorge – Raso de la Bruma – Arure

Starting point: Arure, 826 m (bus stop for lines 1, 6).
Walking time: Arure – Cañada de Jorge 40 min, Cañada de Jorge – Raso de la Bruma – Arure not quite 1½ hrs; total time 2 hrs.
Ascent: Not quite 300 m.
Grade: Pleasant walk along tracks and forest trails with a short 10-min stretch on the Carretera del Centro.

Refreshment: In Arure bar/restaurants.
Combination possible with Walk 18 (via the »Sendero forestal a Las Hayas«, →Walk 20) and with Walk 20.
Tip: The walk can also begin on the Carretera del Centro near the picnic place Raso de la Bruma (sign; between the road junction at Apartacaminos, about 1.5 km away and the road junction Cruce de Las Hayas, about 1.8 km away).

This pleasant half-day walk draws us into the mystifying heart of Gomera – the laurisilva forest – and presents an ideal combination with the even more impressive »Jardín de Las Creces Circuit Route« (Walk 18). Both walks share the aspect of beginning in a pastoral landscape and then entering a primeval forest – especially after rainfall an unforgettable experience!
The starting point for the walk is the upper district of **Arure** (Casas de Acardece) on the main road near the dam wall (10 min by foot along the road from the village centre and the bar »Concita«). Here a road forks off to the right following a huge water conduit passing the man-made lake of the Embalse Arure at the same time. This leads into the valley bearing right then

Arure – the district Casas de Acardece.

forks after 5 min – here straight on ascending the cement road (the right fork is the »Sendero forestal a Las Hayas«, sign). Passing a left fork leading to a house, the now narrow and partially washed-out road leads into a scrub wood to immediately fork again. Continue straight on the main trail and also a few minutes later by bearing right, ascending shortly along a ridge and then entering a lovely laurel wood. Continue straight on the pleasant forestry track to reach a major fork after a few minutes; here again straight on through the gentle valley notch to the nearby former picnic place **Cañada de Jorge**, 970 m. Right (along the left side of the stream bed) a forestry trail continues, forking at the same time – here do not continue along the stream bed but instead ascend to the left. This splendid *camino*, shaded by the thick vegetation of the tropical forest, climbs over a mountain ridge and after a quarter hour merges into the Carretera del Centro (sign »Camino forestal Raso de la Bruma«), near a small picnic place with picnic tables **Raso de la Bruma**, 1070 m.

Continue the route by turning left onto the mountain road and not quite 10 min (700 m) later turn sharply left onto the broad »Camino forestal Raso D. Pedro« (sign; chain barrier). Again enjoying the softness of a forest trail, descend gently through the laurel forest to merge again after not quite half an hour into our approach trail (2 min to the left – Cañada de Jorge). Turn right to return to **Arure**.

20 From Arure to Chipude

Relaxing ramble through the mountain villages above the Valle Gran Rey

Arure – Las Hayas – El Cercado – Chipude

Starting point: Arure, 826 m (bus stop for lines 1, 6).
Destination: The church square of Chipude, 1080 m (bus stop for lines 1, 6 and 7).
Walking time: Arure – Las Hayas a good 1 hr, Las Hayas – El Cercado 1 hr, El Cercado – Chipude ½ hr; total time a good 2½ hrs.
Ascent: A total of about 400 m in ascent with only a little descent.
Grade: Easy, pleasant walk via forestry roads and *caminos*.
Refreshment: Bar/restaurants in Arure, Las Hayas, El Cercado and Chipude.
Alternative: Mountain walkers with stamina can follow an excellent extended route by combining this one with the ascent from La Calera to Arure (→Walk 29).
Combination possible with Walks 13–19, 21–23.
Tip: The walk can also begin or end in the villages of Las Hayas and El Cercado (bus stops for lines 1, 6, 7).

This stimulating walk through the mountain villages above the Valle Gran Rey has a lot to offer: constantly changing scenery, views into the Barranco del Agua and, last but not least, numerous bars and restaurants.

Begin the walk in the village centre of **Arure** near the »Concita« bar. From here ascend the main road for about 10 min to reach the upper district of Casas de Acardece then turn right along a road following a huge water conduit passing along the man-made lake Embalse Arure (afterwards a track continues). 5 min later bear right at the fork onto the »Sendero forestal a Las Hayas« (sign) leading through vineyards into the valley. At the fork next to a couple of palm trees bear left to continue (the right fork makes a short cut). Later the small road narrows into a footpath for a few minutes then broadens back into a road. This leads shortly afterwards through the valley floor in a sharp right-hand bend and then broadens again into a forestry track to continue, bearing left at the first fork, straight on to **Las Hayas**, 1000 m.

In the village, ascend along the main road to the left for a short time then turn right just below the bar/restaurant »La Montaña« onto the cement-paved *camino* which soon becomes cobblestone. The *camino* leads through terraces of palm trees, crosses over a valley floor then ascends leisurely to a small mountain ridge; continue along this to meet an intersecting road after a quarter hour. Now straight on, passing a house, to the next fork 100 m further. Here straight (left) to continue a light ascent and after 20 m passing between palm trees. Ascend in 5 min to another small mountain ridge and then straight on, at first traversing then descending along the edge of the gorge-like Barranco del Agua. Now the most impressive stretch of the route follows: past a small cistern reach a brilliant overlook »balcony« with a gorgeous downward view into the gorge that ends at a cliff wall to the left – to the right enjoy a view reaching far into the Valle Gran Rey. Now continue the descent passing through splendidly-constructed terraces to reach the course of a stream. Afterwards cross through terraces along the valley floor and then another stream course bearing right along the *camino* to ascend to **El Cercado**, 1030 m, reaching the main road directly across from the bar »Maria«.

Follow the street shortly to the right to the bar/restaurant »Victoria« (a few steps further on – the famous potters' workshops) then turn right onto a cement-paved trail below the road continuing into the valley to reach a broad cobblestone road. Descend here to the right and when it ends continue straight on along the *camino*, only to leave this about 50 m on by turning left to ascend along a stepped trail. The broad trail crosses the main road and climbs to a rise. With a view of Chipude, cross to the other side then again over the main road, descending into the Barranco de los Manantiales; on the opposite side ascend again to the main road then turn right passing a wash-house and ascend to a bus stop shelter. Shortly after, a small cobblestone street forks left ascending to the church square of **Chipude**.

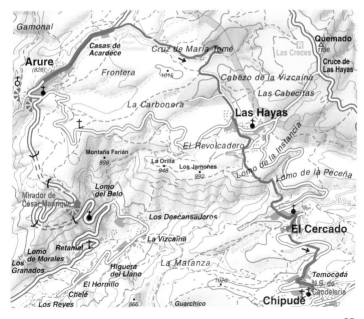

21 From Valle Gran Rey to Las Hayas

Straight shot along a sheer cliff to the renowned Casa Efigenia

Lomo del Balo – Las Hayas – Lomo del Balo

Starting point: Lomo del Balo, 430 m (bus stop for lines 1, 6).
Walking time: Lomo del Balo – Las Hayas 1¾ hrs, Las Hayas – Lomo del Balo 1¾ hrs; total time 3½ hrs.
Ascent: 600 m.
Grade: Very steep and strenuous ascent along a sometimes narrow, somewhat precipitous *camino* requiring absolute sure-footedness and an excellent head for heights. The continued route to Las Hayas lacks a distinct trail. The return is also steep and requires sure-footedness.
Refreshment: Bar/restaurants in Las Hayas, bar in Lomo del Balo.
Alternative: Ascent from La Calera to Lomo del Balo (alternatively, descent from Lomo del Balo to La Calera: use Walk 23 until reaching La Vizcaína, but then continue on the road to reach the starting point of the walk on the main road (1½ hrs; descent from La Vizcaína to La Calera →Walk 17, 1¼ hrs).
Combination possible with Walks 18, 20 and 22.

This walk along the cliff face of the Valle Gran Rey can hardly be matched when it comes to steep: an almost »full-speed-ahead« tour without bends or rest breaks but opening all-the-more spectacular views of the Valle Gran Rey; the sometimes unpleasantly exposed »straightaway« ascends to the plateau of Las Hayas. Walkers preferring to avoid this steep climb should begin the route in Las Hayas.

View from the trail into the Valle Gran Rey.

Begin the walk in **Lomo del Balo**, the Valle Gran Rey's highest village on the main road. Here, where the main road takes a sharp bend (good place to park) a road forks off towards the village districts on the other side of the valley crossing a bridge at the same time. 100 m after the bridge reach a sharp right bend (bridge) and ascend to the left through the boulder-strewn stream bed until about 50 m on turning left onto a steep cobblestone trail and leaving the stream bed behind. This wins in elevation quite quickly. After not quite half an hour, continue along the main trail by bearing left (a nice place for a break to the right) then after a short and slightly exposed traverse ascend steeply again. Shortly after negotiating a few beige/red-coloured steps cut into the rock, a traverse leads to the right over a narrow, precipitous rock ledge that opens lovely downward views into the valley. Afterwards continue ascending mostly steeply. An hour later, shortly after crossing a small stone wall, the worst is over – the *camino* bears right in a traverse towards a *barranco*, then forks a few minutes later and about 50 m before the *barranco* head, after having passed a few undercuts in the rock. Continue along the smaller trail straight on (not to the left further on the main trail) passing a walled-up cave and leaving the *barranco*. Following the traces of a path, continue along the stream bed until reaching an indistinct track crossing the stream bed about 15 min later. Ascend left along this to reach the road between Arure and Las Hayas; turn right and after a few minutes continue along a broad trail that forks off to the right. Always straight on, this merges in **Las Hayas**, 1000 m, with the road that leads in a few minutes to the bar/restaurant »La Montaña« (Casa Efigenia).

Below the bar, turn right onto the *camino* which is cement-paved at first. This leads through terraces of palm trees, crosses over the valley floor and ascends leisurely to a small mountain ridge to meet an intersecting road (¼ hr). Continue straight on, passing a house to reach the next fork 100 m on then fork to the right onto a *camino* (the *camino* straight ahead leads to El Cercado). This crosses a flat, high meadow valley and after not quite 10 min reaches a superb overlook about 10 m to the left of the trail: beyond the canyon-like Barranco del Agua, the view stretches to El Cercado and the Fortaleza. At this spot, a dare-devil path also descends which we will meet again later during our descent, however, remain on the main trail that leads for another good 5 min along the mountain ridge and then gradually begins a steep descent into the Valle Gran Rey. Not quite an hour later, already reaching the height of the first terraces of La Vizcaína, the *camino* crosses a small water channel. Shortly after, reach a fork: to the left a possible descent towards La Calera; but we bear right, shortly descending then continue by bearing right along the main trail which leads pretty much on the level and is soon joined by a large water conduit. Shortly before the bar »Lomo Balo« reach the connecting road; turn right here and return in 5 min to the main road in **Lomo del Balo**.

22 From Valle Gran Rey to Vallehermoso

Colossal crossing from the south to the north –
through terraces, palm groves and evergreen laurisilva forests

La Vizcaína – Las Hayas – Jardín de Las Creces – Pista forestal La Meseta – Vallehermoso

Starting point: La Vizcaína, 420 m (next bus stop for lines 1 and 6 in Lomo del Balo).
Destination: The *plaza* of Vallehermoso, 186 m (bus stop for lines 3, 4, 5, 7).
Walking time: La Vizcaína – Las Hayas 2 hrs, Las Hayas – Jardín de Las Creces 40 min, Jardín de Las Creces – Pista forestal La Meseta a good ¾ hr, Pista forestal La Meseta – Vallehermoso 1¾ hrs; total time 5¼ hrs (from La Calera add 1¼ hrs).
Ascent: 650 m and 900 m in descent.
Grade: Strenuous hike via mostly good but steep trails; physical fitness and sure-

footedness required.
Refreshment: Bar/restaurants in Lomo del Balo, Las Hayas and Vallehermoso.
Alternative: Begin the route in Las Hayas or on the Carretera del Centro at the fork leading to Jardín de Las Creces (sign; between the road junction at Apartacaminos, about 2.3 km away, and the junction at Cruce de Las Hayas, about 1 km away).
Combination possible with Walk 34 (from Pista forestal La Meseta) to Vallehermoso or in the opposite direction to the bar/restaurant »Chorros de Epina«.

The traverse from Valle Gran Rey into the idyllic Vallehermoso Valley belongs to one of the island's grandest scenic displays. During the steep ascent to Las Hayas, enjoy stupendous views of the Valle Gran Rey. Further along the route, experience the wondrous laurel forest of Bosque del Cedro then, descending from here into the centre of the north-west island, enjoy constant views embracing the gentle valley landscapes of Vallehermoso.
The best starting point when using public transportation (bus) is in **Lomo del Balo**, the highest district of Valle Gran Rey on the main road. Where the main road takes a sharp bend (parking possible), a street forks towards the districts on the other side of the valley – after 5 min this leads past the bar »Lomo Balo«. 50 m past the bar, a cobblestone trail forks to the left – this merges later with our ascent route. However, we continue another 5 min along the street until reaching the telephone booth in La Vizcaína. (Walkers ascending to this point from La Calera follow Walk 23 until passing through La Vizcaína and continue along the street for a few minutes until reaching the telephone booth).

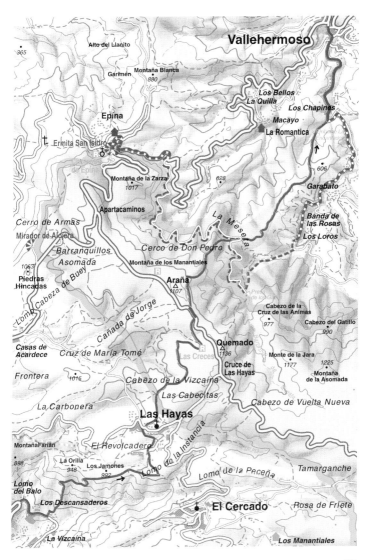

The cobblestone trail to Las Hayas ascends steeply to the left of the telephone booth, leaving the houses of La Vizcaína soon behind. After a few minutes, cross a small water channel then climb steeply, straight on, over a mountain ridge. Only after a further ascent does the trail level out a bit. Not quite a half hour later and after a small left-hand bend, the *camino* leads in a short traverse to the right through the rocks, opening a marvellous panoramic view over the entire Valle Gran Rey sweeping to La Calera. Now ascend steeply again, passing above a power pylon. Steeper stretches mixed with easier stretches follow. After completing three final switchbacks, pass the first overgrown terraces. Shortly after, about 1¼ hours from La Vizcaína, reach the plateau above the Valle Gran Rey and walk along the right-hand rim enjoying views of the dramatic Barranco del Agua and of Chipude with the Fortaleza as backdrop as well as of El Cercado. 5 min later, the main trail bears away from the rim and then meets a major fork after another good 5 min. Keep to the left fork continuing straight on (a *camino* forks sharply to the right towards El Cercado, →Walk 20), to reach **Las Hayas**, 1000 m, a quarter hour later. Merge with the main road immediately below the bar/restaurant »La Montaña« (Casa Efigenia).

Just above the Casa Efigenia, in the next bend in the main road, a street forks off to the left and then ends. Passing to the left of a house, a trail continues – ascend along this always straight on. After 5 min pass to the left of the church then immediately after, pass a cistern. Now the trail becomes a path leading straight on, sweeping to the left and entering a scrub wood (50 m on – a national park sign). At the fork 35 m after the national park sign bear right. The path leads pretty much on the level through the lovely forest and after a good 5 min merges into a broad forestry trail (signs »Carretera dorsal / Las Hayas«); turn right here. A good 20 min later reach a small picnic place surrounded by a lovely laurel forest – **Jardín de Las Creces**, 1040 m (tap with spring water) and merges 5 min later in the Carretera del Centro (Carretera dorsal).

Follow the mountain road for a few minutes to the left and then at the next left-hand bend bear right onto an almost level path. This leads in a lovely 10-min traverse through the laurel forest to a rocky clearing. From here descend in a bend to a mountain ridge then continue the descent along this towards Vallehermoso. In the interim, the route leads along the crest of the ridge before again winding in a steep descent to the **Pista forestal La Meseta**, 750 m.

Cross this forestry track (to the right, a pleasant descent using Walk 34 to Vallehermoso) and continue the route along the mountain ridge. The narrow, and later on somewhat precipitous and more overgrown trail ascends for a short time and then leads along the right flank of the ridge with a gorgeous view of the Barranco de la Cuesta. After not quite half an hour reach a plateau of light-coloured sand with a view and then descend for a good

Vallehermoso – the north-west's main town charms with idyllic valley landscapes.

5 min to a saddle. Skirt around to the right of the next crag on the ridge. A good 5 min after the saddle reach a fork on the ridgeline (a very fine view of Vallehermoso with Roque El Cano; straight ahead on the ridgeline – a large, drawn-out rock massif). Take the descending path to the left that soon returns to the crest of the mountain ridge and after 5 min, about 100 m before a saddle at the foot of the drawn-out massif, make a sharp left onto the slope. 5 min later, crossing over a covered water channel at the end, meet a road – here left, descending to the road between Vallehermoso and Los Loros in 20 min (merging 50 m below a transformer pylon at a sharp bend in the road). Follow the road to the left then 20 min later next to the bar/restaurant »Garajonay«, turn left onto the shopping street to finally reach the *plaza* of **Vallehermoso** shortly after.

23 From Valle Gran Rey to El Cercado

Extensive circuit route to the pottery village above the Valle Gran Rey

(La Calera –) La Vizcaína – El Cercado – La Matanza – Ermita de los Reyes (– La Calera)

Starting point: La Calera, 50 m (bus stop for lines 1, 6) or La Vizcaína, 420 m (next bus stop for lines 1 and 6 in Lomo del Balo, 430 m).
Walking time: La Calera – Ermita de los Reyes ½ hr, Ermita de los Reyes – La Vizcaína ¾ hr, La Vizcaína – El Cercado 1¾ hrs, El Cercado – La Matanza ¾ hr, La Matanza – Ermita de los Reyes 1¾ hrs, Ermita de los Reyes – La Calera ½ hr; total time from La Calera 6 hrs (La Vizcaína – Ermita de los Reyes 1¾ hrs shorter).
Ascent: From La Calera about 1050 m in ascent and descent, from La Vizcaína not quite 400 m less ascent.
Grade: Strenuous, but not very difficult hike along fairly broad *caminos*, unfortunately often stony, especially during the descent.
Refreshment: Bar/restaurants in La Calera, La Vizcaína and in El Cercado.
Combination possible with Walks 20, 24 and 26.
Tip: The walk can also end in the village of El Cercado, 1030 m (bus stop for lines 1 and 6).

The circuit route presented here and starting from the cultivated terraces of the Valle Gran Rey presents walkers with a number of possible variations: those preferring a pleasant half-day's tour can begin their walk either at the Ermita de los Reyes or in La Vizcaína (15 min from the bus stop in Lomo del Balo) and then return by bus from El Cercado. On the other hand, hikers with plenty of stamina will choose La Calera as their starting point not to miss the chance to experience the impressive descent via the La Matanza pasturage.

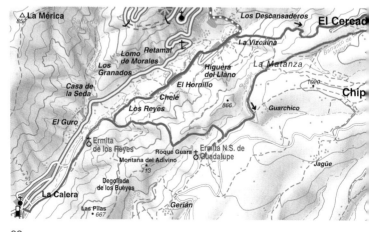

The Ermita de los Reyes – pivotal and radial point for walks in the Valle Gran Rey.

Across from the Cepsa petrol station near the road bridge in **La Calera** descend the steps to the stream bed of Barranco del Valle Gran Rey then follow the track ascending along the right flank of the *barranco*. After a good 20 min pass a dark-coloured cliff wall. Just after this a little trail forks to the right and continues over a rock ledge then a few minutes later reaches the pretty **Ermita de los Reyes**, 150 m, located a bit above the valley floor (if you chose to continue along the stream bed, you can reach the chapel by ascending right via the stone steps after a total of ½ hr).

Behind the chapel a delightful cobblestone trail continues, lightly ascending between palm tree terraces and colourful gardens. Not quite 10 min later another stone-paved *camino* forks to the right (our return route later on); however, remain on the slope trail leading straight on. This merges some minutes later into an asphalt street near **Chelé**, then shortly after this, forks in **El Hornillo** – continue here to the right. A good half hour from the chapel, the street takes a sharp bend to the right (at the next left-hand bend – the bar/*bodegón* »La Vizcaína«). To the left (straight on) there is a short-cut possible along a cobblestone trail that meets up with the street some minutes later in **La Vizcaína**. Continue along this for a few minutes more until reaching a reed-blanketed lay-by where a stone-paved stepped trail ascends to the right (¾ hr from Ermita de los Reyes; soon after, the street crosses in a left bend to the other side of the valley and then merges with the main road in Lomo del Balo after a total of ¼ hr).

The La Mantanza pasturage.

The steps merge immediately into a cobblestone trail – ascend along this (red circle marking). A few minutes later bear right at the fork to continue the climb and then a good 10 min after leaving the street reach a waterworks; here, the *camino* bears left along the slope. The somewhat bumpy but mostly pleasant trail continues a steady ascent then forks after a good quarter hour: remain on the broad main trail that leads to the left and on the level through a small, gentle *barranco* gap (the extremely steep cliff trail forking right at the red double-arrow marking to the La Matanza pasturage is closed due to a rock slide) then climb again immediately after. With fantastic downward views of the Valle Gran Rey and later of the Barranco del Agua reach the crest of the ridge by a first house (1½ hrs from Vizcaína). Ascending the broad road straight on, reach the main street just across from the bar »Maria« in **El Cercado**, 1030 m (bus stop for lines 1, 6, 7).

After a good long break follow the street to the right passing a pottery maker's until reaching a bus stop shelter at the sharp right-hand bend. Here right to descend the broad cobblestone road. This crosses over the *barranco* in a few minutes then 100 m (50 m after the sharp right-hand bend) and just after the houses, bear to the right onto a distinct trail that pleasantly descends into the valley. Soon leaving the last houses of the village behind continue straight on, descending along the left flank of the Barranco de la Matanza. Later change over to the right valley flank then soon after, again towards the stream bed. Two trails continue parallel to the stream bed: the left trail descends near the stream bed into the beautiful palm-planted valley; however, we follow the straight somewhat better-maintained right-hand trail leading along the slope above the valley. The two trails eventually merge again on the slope at about middle height. From this point it is only 5 min to reach the valley floor and the pasturage **La Matanza**, 780 m, where the closed cliff trail to La Vizcaína forks to the right (lovely spot for a rest with a first-rate view of the Valle Gran Rey).

The continued route to La Calera is identical with Walk 16: remain on the straight main trail – the distinct path leads along the left-hand slope of the Barranco de Argaga which begins near La Matanza, always following along or near an abandoned water channel. After 10 min pass below a property with vineyards. 15 min later take a sharp right onto a distinct cobblestone trail (cairns; straight on the channel trail leads to the little **Ermita de Nuestra Señora de Guadalupe**, 750 m, 20 min there and back. After 10 min the *camino* crosses over the Barranco de Argaga and continues straight ahead on the other side bearing left in an easy ascent to reach the crest of the ridge above the Valle Gran Rey and then forks. Turn right onto the cobblestone trail leading towards the valley and opening superb views of the middle Valle Gran Rey. After not quite 1 hr, below one of the first houses, the stony *camino* meets up with a broad intersecting trail – here left to reach **Ermita de los Reyes**, 150 m. From here return along the approach route to **La Calera**.

What starts off as a gully, ends as a gargantuan gorge: Barranco de Argaga near La Mantanza.

24 From Ermita de los Reyes to La Vizcaína

Awe-inspiring and precipitous walk above the Valle Gran Rey

(La Calera –) Ermita de los Reyes – crest of the ridge above the Valle Gran Rey – La Vizcaína – El Hornillo – Ermita de los Reyes (– La Calera)

Location: La Calera, 50 m (bus stop for lines 1, 6).
Starting point: Ermita de los Reyes, 150 m (only accessible by foot: a good

5 min from the main street in El Guro or ½ hr from La Calera, →Walk 23).
Walking time: Ermita de los Reyes – the crest of the ridge 1¼ hrs, crest of the ridge – El Hornillo 1¼ hrs, El Hornillo – Ermita de los Reyes ¾ hr; total time 3¼ hrs (from La Calera add 1 hr).
Ascent: 550 m.
Grade: Difficult hike requiring sure-footedness and a good head for heights: the traverse along the rock ridge is very narrow and exposed; the continued descent to La Vizcaína is sometimes just as precipitous and very steep. Do not attempt the route after rainfall or during strong winds!
Refreshment: Bar/restaurants in La Calera.
Combination possible with Walks 16, 23, 26 and 27.

High up, along the sheer cliff wall above the middle Valle Gran Rey, follows the most spectacular and panoramic stretch of this hike, leading for a good quarter hour over an extremely narrow and exposed ledge of rock with constant downward views of the valley lying hundreds of metres below. Definitely not an experience for walkers with weak nerves!

The first leg of the tour is identical with Walk 25: from the **Ermita de los Reyes** follow the trail leading into the valley and not quite 10 min later turn right onto the ascending *camino* (sign »Kirchenpfad«). The *camino* soon bears left to ascend to a mountain ridge and then continues the ascent along this. Now always remain on the somewhat rocky but mostly broad main trail and after a good hour reach the **crest of the ridge**, 658 m, above the Valle Gran Rey.

The trail forks just on the other side of the crest. Bear left continuing on the main trail (the right fork leads to the plateau Las Pilas and to Tequergenche; →Walk 26) into the Barranco de Argaga then about 50 m on, fork to the left onto a very indistinct path. This lightly ascends leading to a prominent **ridge gap** with a couple of rock walls (10 min), hard to miss despite the numerous goat trails (directly after the ridge gap, a long, drawn-out rock face).

Enjoying a fantastic view of the Valle Gran Rey continue along the now distinct trail descending in a couple of tight zigzags. Afterwards, the trail bears

Underway along the fascinating ledge high above the Valle Gran Rey.

to the right and soon leads off onto a level reddish rock ledge continuing into the valley beneath a remarkable cliff face. After a good quarter hour the narrow, exposed traverse along the ledge comes to an end. The trail now descends in a wide bend along some precipitous stretches to a projecting rock then continues descending to the right into a scree-filled gully leaving this again 40 m on by turning to the right and finally along tight bends descends to the well-maintained terraces in La Vizcaína. Near the first houses, the *camino* becomes a lovely stopped trail descending steeply then levels out at the end at a right-to-left bend finally reaching the main street in **La Vizcaína**, 400 m.

Descend along this to the left and a good quarter hour later at the road junction in **El Hornillo** bear left (straight on). A few minutes later at the end of the street turn right onto a *camino* that passes along the foot of a hole-riddled dark-coloured rock massif. After not quite 10 min, our approach trail merges from the left – reach the **Ermita de los Reyes** a few minutes later.

25 From Valle Gran Rey via La Matanza to El Cercado

Ascent from the Valle Gran Rey to the picturesque mountain villages on the border of the national park

(La Calera –) Ermita de los Reyes – La Matanza – El Cercado

Location: La Calera, 50 m (bus stop for lines 1, 6).
Starting point: Ermita de los Reyes, 150 m (only accessible by foot: a good 5 min from the main street in El Guro or ½ hr from La Calera, →Walk 23).
Destination: El Cercado, 1030 m (bus stop for lines 1, 6, 7).
Walking time: Ermita de los Reyes – the crest of the ridge 1¼ hrs, crest of the ridge – La Matanza 1 hr, La Matanza – El Cercado 1 hr; total time 3¼ hrs (from La Calera add ½ hr).
Ascent: Not quite 1000 m.
Grade: Not very difficult; however perse-

verance and sure-footedness are required for the route leading along a sometimes stony *camino*.
Refreshment: Bar/restaurants in La Calera and in El Cercado.
Alternatives: From La Matanza, a possible ascent to Chipude (1 hr) – the trail forks to the right shortly after the dam wall and ascends above the Barranco de los Manantiales to the main road then reaches the church square a few minutes later. – Return possible via Walk 17.
Combination possible with Walks 20, 24 and 26.

Here is yet another ascent from the Valle Gran Rey to the mountain villages at the edge of the Garajonay National Park: the route is identical with the descent described in Walk 23, but is included here because of its popularity as well as the combinations possible when walking the route in this direction.

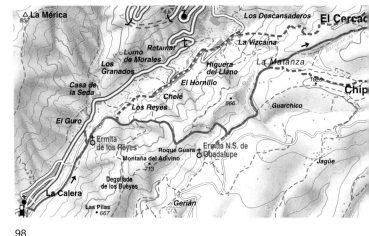

From **Ermita de los Reyes** follow the trail leading into the valley. Not quite 10 min later, near some houses, a *camino* turns to the right (sign »Kirchenpfad«) that ascends for a short time along a *barranco* gully and then turns left to a mountain ridge continuing the climb along this. The trail forks about 25 min from the chapel. Remain on the ascending main trail that continues mostly along the right flank of the steep mountain ridge. This is fairly stony but nevertheless good for walking. After a good three quarters hour, pass a small house to the right being used as a stable then at the fork shortly after ascend to the left. About 20 min later reach the **crest of the ridge**, 658 m, above the Valle Gran Rey and on the other side, the trail forks.

Channel trail between Barranco de Argaga and La Matanza.

Bear left along the main trail (to the right – the route to the Las Pilas plateau; →Walk 26). Lightly descend to the Barranco de Argaga then climb up on the other side in a good 10 min to an abandoned water channel which the *camino* then crosses: to the right along the channel you can reach the **Ermita de Nuestra Señora de Guadalupe**, 750 m, in 10 min. However, we swing sharply left onto the channel trail (the path leads sometimes in, sometimes along the channel), ascending pleasantly above the Barranco de Argaga. After a quarter hour cross a boulder-strewn stream bed then another quarter hour later reach the stone houses of the **La Matanza** pasturage, 780 m situated at the *barranco* head. The water channel ends here at a small inconspicuous dam wall; immediately after, a cliff trail forks left crossing a small gap (lovely rest area with a view of the Valle Gran Rey) then descends to La Vizcaína, but is closed due to a rock slide.

Continue the walk along the main trail towards the valley head. 30 m on, this forks after the small dam wall: the right fork leads to Chipude, but our trail crosses the valley floor and then ascends along the left flank bearing slightly left and traversing the slope passing above pretty terraces. Not quite a half hour later, the *camino* levels off slightly and then forks shortly after at the valley floor. Here, take the cobblestone trail leading along the right flank and soon pass the first houses to ascend straight on to the main road in **El Cercado**.

26 Tequergenche, 515 m

Panoramic walk above the Valle Gran Rey

(La Calera –) Ermita de los Reyes – Degollada de los Bueyes – Las Pilas – Tequergenche and back

Location: La Calera, 50 m (bus stop for lines 1, 6).

Starting point: Ermita de los Reyes, 150 m (only accessible by foot: a good 5 min from the main street in El Guro or ½ hr from La Calera, →Walk 23).

Walking time: Ermita de los Reyes – the crest of the ridge 1¼ hrs, crest – Las Pilas ¾ hr, Las Pilas – Tequergenche – Las Pilas 1½ hrs, Las Pilas – Ermita de los Reyes 1¾ hrs; total time 5¼ hrs (without Tequergenche 3¾ hrs).

Ascent: About 800 m.

Grade: Not very difficult, however sure-footedness required; along the Pilas plateau sometimes without a distinct path.

Refreshment: Bar/restaurants in La Calera.

Alternative: Descent from Degollada de los Bueyes via the Leche path (only for the experienced, sure-footed mountain hiker with an excellent head for heights and craving adventure; pay close attention to stepping stones and cairns since goat tracks confuse the route, otherwise stumbles and blunders are more than a certainty): The panoramic, increasingly ticklish path mostly leads lightly descending along the steep slope high above the Valle Gran Rey and after 15 min passes

»Ciro's caves«, once used as goat stables. Not quite ¾ hr later, about 20 min before Ermita de los Reyes, the path meets up with the more popular ascent route.

Combination possible with Walks 16, 24 and 25.

This walk along the Las Pilas tableland, which separates the Valle Gran Rey from the Argaga Gorge, counts as one of the most panoramic excursions described in this guide: from the plateau to its »pillar« Tequergenche, enjoy breathtaking downward views of the Argaga Beach and of Vueltas, La Playa as well as the lower Valle Gran Rey. Also gaze over wide expanses of the island's south-west.

The ascent at first follows Walk 25: from **Ermita de los Reyes** take the trail leading into the valley then not quite 10 min later turn right onto a *camino* that, in just less than an hour, ascends to the **crest of the ridge**, 658 m, above the Valle Gran Rey.

Downward view over the rooftops of Vueltas from the rim of the Las Pilas plateau.

Here turn right and away from the main trail to follow the smaller trail leading along the left flank of the ridge. After a few minutes this approaches the ridgeline again and a gap but then continues traversing to the left along the slope to reach, about 25 min later and after a slight descent, a broad saddle of red sand, 588 m, with a lovely view of La Calera. Following the cairns to the left of the ridge, reach another saddle a good 5 min later: **Degollada de los Bueyes**, 581 m (the sharp right fork is the Leche path, →Alternative). Continue along the ridge, skirting to the left around the rocky outcrop and after 10 min below two stone houses reach the plateau **Las Pilas**, 667 m. Passing to the left of the two houses, a path continues along a drystone wall. The path leads past an old threshing yard then continues towards the middle of the plateau and a small rocky rise on the other side of which more ruins of stone houses can be found. If you prefer not to continue on to Tequergenche, pick out a pretty place for a break and enjoy the view of Gerián and the Fortaleza.

To continue the route, walk along the left rim of the gently-sloped plateau without a distinct path. Past a house with a threshing yard, descend through overgrown terraces to a saddle, 487 m, where a path ascends to **Tequergenche** – this plunges in a sheer drop to the south-east towards Playa de Argaga. After the excursion to the peak, return to the last saddle and ascend from there bearing left along the edge of the Las Pilas plateau now enjoying spectacular downward views of the mouth of the Barranco del Valle Gran Rey, from Vueltas' harbour all the way to La Calera! Steady on along the path following the plateau rim catch another view of the lower districts with the Barranco de Arure. Past the cross dedicated to Reuß, return to the north-west rim of the plateau to complete the 1½ hr-long circuit route. Directly beneath the two houses meet up with the approach trail to return along this to **Ermita de los Reyes**.

27 Barranco de Argaga – from Vueltas to Gerián

Dare-devil ascent through the craggy labyrinth of the Argaga Gorge

Vueltas – Playa de Argaga – Barranco de Argaga – Gerián – Ermita N.S. de Guadalupe – Ermita de los Reyes (– La Calera/Vueltas)

Starting point: The harbour of Vueltas, 5 m (bus stop for lines 1, 6).
Destination: La Calera, 50 m (bus stop for lines 1, 6).
Walking time: Vueltas – Playa de Argaga ¼ hr, Playa de Argaga – Gerián 3 hrs, Gerián – Ermita N.S. de Guadalupe 20 min, Ermita N.S. de Guadalupe – the crest of the ridge ½ hr, crest – Ermita de los Reyes 1 hr, Ermita de los Reyes – La Calera ½ hr; total time 5½ hrs (to Vueltas add not quite ½ hr).
Ascent: About 900 m.
Grade: Just as risky as it is demanding, the ascent through the Barranco de Argaga requires sure-footedness and stamina as well as an excellent head for heights. The climb leads mostly through a craggy and extremely perplexing terrain (now and again easy stretches

of scrambling requiring the use of handholds), but is fortunately so well-marked that only seldom does the continuation need clarification. The return route to the Valle Gran Rey follows with very little difficulty. During periods of unstable weather and after rainfall never attempt to climb into the gorge!
Refreshment: Bar/restaurants in the Valle Gran Rey.
Alternatives: From Gerián, a possible ascent along a track to Chipude (1¼ hrs). – From the trail crossing on the abandoned water channel, you can follow the channel to the right to walk via the La Matanza pasturage to El Cercado or to Chipude (→Walk 25 or Walk 16).
Combination possible with Walks 24 and 26 (from the crest of the ridge above the Valle Gran Rey).

The demanding ascent through the chasm-like Argaga Gorge is one of the greatest walking adventures that Gomera has to offer – in continuous up-and-down climbing, steep rocky inclines must be scrambled over, canyon-like crevices bypassed and precipitous ledges crossed – this is accompanied by a constant fretful search for the continued ascent: preordained by a rock chaos and apparently bestowed by pure chance. Experienced, adventurous mountain lovers will find boundless delights in this ascent, other walkers will soon begin to long for this strenuous circuit route to finally come to an end!

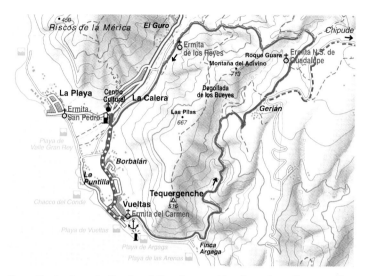

From the harbour in **Vueltas** follow the road leading along the coastline then below the cliff face of Tequergenche to reach the **Playa de Argaga** in a quarter hour with the holiday and meditation centre »Argayall« (straight on along the coast, a possible excursion to the Playa de las Arenas, 10 min). In front of the Sanyassins' »Place of Light« turn left on a road leading into the Barranco de Argaga (note: the entire lower *barranco* is private property - if the gate is closed, you must retrace and then ascend directly through the *barranco* until reaching a rock barrier on the *barranco* floor in a good 5 min; by scrambling to the left over this you will once again meet the road). 10 min later and shortly after passing the fruit garden of the Finca Argayall to the left, the road crosses over the *barranco* floor.

Here, turn right along the *barranco* floor (cairns; red spot markings) ascending for a few minutes to reach a point where the *barranco* narrows next to a concrete foundation. Left over the red rocks then along a stone wall descend again to the *barranco* floor. After a short stretch along the right side, ascend to the right of the *barranco* floor on a distinct *camino*. This skirts around to the right of a rock step on the *barranco* floor with a water reservoir then ascends over scree bearing left to reach a terrace. From here ascend over scree to the right to reach the third and highest terrace and cross over this to the left. Just before it ends, ascend shortly to the left and follow the rim of the *barranco* to reach a small dam wall. Along the dam wall cross over to the left side of the *barranco*. Soon after, past a canyon-like cut in the *barranco*, continue over rocks then pass between two terrace walls to return to the right side of the *barranco*.

Then, above the terraces (follow the red spot markings), ascend through a steep gully, mostly rocky but with patches of scree as well (light scrambles, l). After about 10 min, at the upper end of the gully, the way is blocked by a reddish outcrop of rock. Climbing out of the gully to the left, follow a narrow *camino* that leads along a ledge at the foot of a cliff above the chasm-like *barranco*. Not quite 5 min later descend again to the left to the stream bed, to reach this directly above the ledge of a waterfall (about 1 hr from Playa de Argaga).

Continue a good 100 m along the *barranco* floor then turn left between terrace walls to leave it behind. Crossing terraces and bearing right, at the end passing under a palm tree and two water conduits, return to the *barranco* floor only to leave it again some metres further on to the right in order to skirt around the steep ledge that follows. After another few metres, along the *barranco* floor, climb over a rock wall to another terrace. From here ascend steeply, at the same time bearing right, and sometimes following an abandoned water channel to reach some cliff caves. Past the caves, continue the rocky ascent crossing over a rock barrier to the right then climbing about 10 m through a gully only to leave this again by ascending left using stepping stones. Now bear left ascending steeply to the foot of a small but long cliff face along which we continue the ascent to the right. Cross over two water conduits (below a large cave). Shortly after, again using stepping stones, climb over a high rock barrier. Bearing to the right pass more caves until reaching a cliff wall across from which and slightly below a large cave can be seen. Now left along the cliff wall, continuing over a reddish rock ledge, crossing another water conduit and then reaching a spot below a huge overhanging rock – a good place to take a break (about 2 hrs from Playa de Argaga). From here enjoy a stunning view stretching over the Barranco de Argaga to the sea, which still seems surprisingly near.

Shortly after the cave, the *camino* ascends steeply to the right to reach the foot of a mountain spur. Bearing left, a traverse above the once-again nearby *barranco* floor follows. Pass a couple of pines then cross a field of scree to reach a terrace, then 5 m before a palm tree, ascend steeply bearing right, at the end bearing left, to cultivated terraces. Along these follow the steeply ascending *camino* to the right (avoid the slide-damaged stretch by skirting left over the terraces), to continue above the terraces into the valley. After some minutes the main trail ascends the slope in a series of tight bends. This leads later, about at the height of the palm trees, following a long bend to the right, then to the left, to ascend to the plateau with the hamlet of **Gerián**, 700 m.

Along the left edge of the plateau and past the houses, the *camino* continues (ignore the track to the right towards Chipude). Soon the **Ermita de**

Shortly before the hamlet of Gerián – the Barranco de Argaga can be seen to the left of the photo.

Nuestra Señora de Guadalupe, 750 m, appears before us; to reach this, follow along a water channel, bearing left at a fork. From the little chapel enthroned on the spur of Roque de Guara, enjoy a delightful downwards view of the now fairly tame Barranco de Argaga.

Remain on the trail leading straight on, traversing the slope above an abandoned water channel. This leads in easy up-and-down walking along the channel, then crosses this 5 min later (the channel continues to La Matanza). The further route to La Calera is identical with Walk 16: descend along the *camino* to the floor of the Barranco de Argaga and cross over to the other side by bearing left, then straight on ascending to a fork on the crest of the ridge above the Valle Gran Rey. Here follow the cobblestone trail leading right and into the valley opening lovely views of the middle Valle Gran Rey. Not quite 1 hr later, below one of the first houses, the bumpy *camino* merges with a broad intersecting trail; here left to reach **Ermita de los Reyes**, 150 m, in not quite 10 min. From here to the main street in El Guro or descend through the *barranco* to **La Calera**.

28 Barranco de Arure

Idyllic, short walk to the waterfall near El Guro

El Guro – Barranco de Arure – Salto de Agua – El Guro

Starting point: El Guro, 160 m, district of Valle Gran Rey on the main road (bus stop for lines 1 and 6) not quite 2 km above La Calera. To walk from La Calera to El Guro, follow the track along the right side of the Barranco del Valle Gran Rey until reaching the height of the Ermita de los Reyes then continue through the reeds and rushes, afterwards via steps to ascend to the main road in El Guro (a good ½ hr from La Calera).

Walking time: El Guro – waterfall 1¼ hrs, return 1 hr; total time 2¼ hrs.
Ascent: Not quite 200 m.
Grade: Mostly easy, short walk that nevertheless follows stretches requiring sure-footedness and some light scrambling. The trail is often overgrown and indistinct (rushes and reeds, blackberry undergrowth). Not to be attempted during or after heavy rainfall!
Refreshment: Bar/restaurants in La Calera.

This popular walk in the Barranco de Arure presents Gomera as from a picture book: beginning in the artists' village of El Guro, the walk passes cultivated terraces and majestic basalt cliffs in the idyllic tributary valley of the Valle Gran Rey. At the end of the trail (almost impossible to walk after heavy rainfall) reach a waterfall tumbling 15 metres down into a fabulous rocky basin. The trail is often very tiring and indistinct – when in doubt, simply walk directly along the stream bed.

From the fork of the steps to Ermita de los Reyes at the beginning of the car park right of the road, ascend a good 100 m along the main road until a broad cobblestone trail (railings) forks to the left, crossing a stream bed with reeds and rushes. This ascends along steps towards **El Guro** and levels off 5 min later at a little house with a triangular window. Here the trail forks three ways: take the sharp right-hand fork continuing along the *camino* and at the same time leave the last houses of the village behind then soon traverse the slope along the foot of a beautiful basalt cliff into the valley. 50 m after the basalt cliff, the trail forks. Bearing left, ascend lightly following the yellow / blue / yellow markings to then descend to a stream bed a few minutes later (some easy scrambling). Here left, following the markings and ascending (you can also cross over the stream, climb steeply on the other side, then left and, at the end, along a bulky, black conduit return to the stream). After about a 5-min tiring stretch through (or right next to) the stream bed, the bulky, black conduit appears to the right of the stream (→return route). Continue for not quite another 5 min in the stream bed then next to a large tilted boulder block (palm tree) ascend left on the now red-marked path. After a short stretch above the stream bed, the path crosses over to the right bank. Soon after, the path returns to the left bank then ascends near some palm trees shortly but steeply over terrace walls. Continuing parallel to the stream, pass under a palm tree then descend again to the stream (1 hr from El Guro) to cross over to the other bank. Soon after, return directly to the stream bed following this to the **waterfall**, 300 m, (a good 10 min).

The names of many walkers are inscribed for eternity on the sheer, partially overhanging cliff walls; the pool at the base offers an opportunity to cool off.

At first the return route is identical with the approach. After about a half hour, the bulky conduit appears to the left with a path forking along it. This leads on the level beneath a small basalt cliff with palm trees. Afterwards the path continues along an old water channel (directly beneath the cliff wall) then forks after a few minutes (distinct marking on a boulder block). Descend along the path that swings to the right then continue left at the next fork above the terraces. Now it is not much further to the main road; follow this to the right to return to **El Guro**.

The rock basin with the waterfall.

29 La Mérica, 857 m

Panoramic high ramble above the Valle Gran Rey

La Calera – Riscos de la Mérica – La Mérica – Arure and back

Starting point: La Calera, 50 m (bus stop for lines 1, 6).
Walking time: La Calera – Riscos de la Mérica 1¼ hrs; Riscos de la Mérica – La Mérica ½ hr, La Mérica – Arure 1 hr, return 2 hrs; total time 4¾ hrs.
Ascent: 900 m.
Grade: Mostly an easy hike despite the steep ascent and descent, nevertheless requiring physical fitness and sure-footed-ness.
Refreshment: Bar/restaurants in La Calera and in Arure.
Alternatives: The route can also begin or end in Arure, 826 m (→Walk 30; bus stop for lines 1 and 6).
Combination possible with Walks 19, 20, 31 and 33 (from Arure).

From La Calera a steep *camino real* winds upwards to the La Mérica plateau where the Playa de Valle Gran Rey lies far below. During the sometimes somewhat monotonous but pleasant stretch along the drawn-out tableland enjoy grandiose views of the steep coastline and the Taguluche Valley – a very popular tour that walkers often prefer to start at Arure – avoiding the ascent from La Calera and only desending to there.

Begin the walk in **La Calera** at the turn-off of the road to La Playa. Between the bars »Parada« and »Plaza« follow the broad steps then turn right immediately onto the next set of steps to soon reach the village street. Continue the climb along the street bearing left at the next fork and passing the pension »Bella Cabellos« after some minutes. Just afterwards and past the stream bed crossing, a stepped trail turns to the left from which at the same time our *camino* to Arure forks left through the stream bed

(wooden board with a trail plan). The *camino* ascends in easy zig-zags, opening an increasingly panoramic view of the Valle Gran Rey. After a total of half an hour a trail also ascending from La Calera merges from the left – the *camino* climbs somewhat steeper now while the terrain becomes rockier. A good quarter hour later a distinct path forks left at a basalt cliff and leads to an overlook with a view of the delta at the mouth of the Barranco del Valle Gran Rey. Back on the main trail, finally reach the La Mérica plateau. Here, directly after the last switchback, a distinct path forks to the left leading in about 10 min to the rim of the sheer cliff wall **Riscos de la Mérica** – a splendid place for a break with a superb downwards view of La Playa and Playa del Inglés.

View over La Calera to Vueltas.

Returning to the main trail, 5 min later pass a solitary, dilapidated house and an old circular threshing yard. The trail continues ascending over the gently sloped and terraced tableland to reach a cistern a quarter hour later and another house ruins at a group of crags. After yet another 5 min a path forks left to the survey post on the peak **La Mérica**.

After the excursion to the peak, what is probably the prettiest stretch of the walk begins: this leads along the right-hand side of the ridge through crags and past caves (goat stables) to reach a red-coloured eroded terrain and then passes a black wall of lava. After 20 min the *camino* crosses over to the left side of the ridge but then returns to the right side to lead past a goat corral. Some minutes later the *camino* merges into a road which continues to **Arure**, 826 m, near the end presenting splendid views of the valley basin of Taguluche. Shortly past the first houses, about 100 m from the main road, we recommend a detour (left under the aqueduct) to the **Mirador del Santo**, 800 m, presenting a breath-taking downwards view of the savage coastline between Taguluche and the Galión Mountains – one of the island's most impressive overlooks!

30 The »Royal« Valle Gran Rey Circuit

Extensive circumambulation of the Valle Gran Rey – for Herculean hikers only!

La Calera – Ermita de los Reyes – La Matanza – El Cercado – Las Hayas – Arure – La Mérica – La Calera

During the ascent, enjoy a wonderful view of the Valle Gran Rey.

Starting point: La Calera, 50 m (bus stop for lines 1 and 6).

Walking time: La Calera – Ermita de los Reyes ½ hr, Ermita – the crest of the ridge 1¼ hrs, crest of the ridge – La Matanza 1 hr, La Matanza – El Cercado 1 hr, El Cercado – Las Hayas ¾ hr, Las Hayas – Arure 1 hr, Arure – La Mérica ¾ hr, La Mérica – La Calera 1¼ hrs; total time 7½ hrs.

Ascent: About 1300 m.

Grade: Extremely long and strenuous mountain hike requiring sure-footedness and plenty of stamina.

Refreshment: Bar/restaurants in La Calera, El Cercado, Las Hayas and Arure.

Alternatives: The hike can also begin in La Vizcaína (→Walk 23) or in Lomo del Balo (→Walk 21 or 22; not quite as long). Also the hike can begin or end in El Cercado, Las Hayas and Arure (all three with bus stops for lines 1 and 6).

Without exaggeration, this hike has earned the title »The King's Route of the Valle Gran Rey«. Within a single day, the physically fit and early-rising hiker can experience most of the highpoints offered by the routes along the »Valley of the Grand King«.

Across from the Cepsa petrol station in **La Calera**, descend the steps to reach the track on the opposite side of the valley then ascend along this for a good 20 min until, past a dark-coloured cliff wall, a small trail forks to the right. This leads over a rock outcrop to the marvellously-situated **Ermita de los Reyes**, 150 m (→Walk 23).

The continued route to El Cercado is identical with Walk 25: remain on the trail leading into the valley then not quite 10 min later, immediately after passing a few houses, turn right onto an ascending *camino* (sign »Kirchenpfad«). Soon bearing left, this climbs to a mountain ridge then continues the ascent along this. Remain on the stony but mostly broad main trail to reach, after a good hour, the **crest of the ridge**, 658 m, over the Valle Gran Rey.

Continue left on the main trail (to the right – the fork to Walk 26), leading fairly level along the other side of the ridge into the valley and crossing the Barranco de Argaga after a quarter hour. On the other side, ascend in a

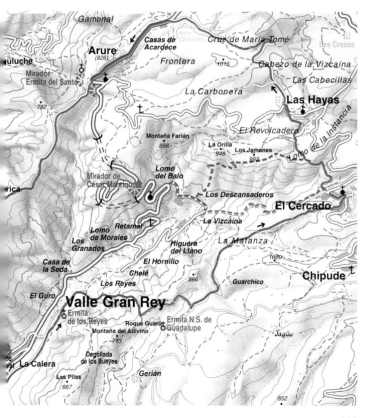

good 10 min to an abandoned water channel that crosses the *camino*. Turn sharply left onto the channel trail leading above the Barranco de Argaga then cross over a rocky stream bed to reach, another quarter hour later, the stone houses of the pasturage **La Matanza**, 780 m located at the head of the *barranco* (to the left a commanding view over the Valle Gran Rey).

The main trail continues into the valley, at the same time changing over to the left flank of the valley (to the right, a trail forks to Chipude) this ascends further bearing slightly left and traversing the slope. After not quite half an hour the trail levels out a bit then forks some minutes later at the valley floor. Here continue on the cobblestone trail leading on the right flank of the valley, soon passing the first houses and ascending to the main street in **El Cercado**, 1030 m (bus stop for lines 1, 6, 7).

Follow the street for a short time to the left to the bar »Maria« then fork off diagonally opposite onto the descending *camino* which bears right. This descends in drawn-out bends (after a few minutes bear left at a fork, then shortly after right or, also possible, straight on) and after a quarter hour crosses over a lovely, terraced valley floor. Afterwards, the *camino* leads left over terraces (superb view of the Valle Gran Rey) then crosses another *barranco* floor to ascend on the other side directly along the rim of the striking Barranco del Agua and on to the next mountain ridge. Continue straight on in steady up-and-down walking, traversing the slope along the trail (at the first houses, crossing a street) to meet the main street in **Las Hayas**, 1000 m, next to the bar/restaurant »La Montaña«.

Shortly before El Cercado – the first destination of the journey.

Backwards view of Mirador del Santo and to Arure.

Now descend about 50 m along the street then turn right onto the broad, at first asphalt-paved, forestry track to Arure. Follow this always straight on and after a good quarter hour remain on the main track that descends in a right-hand bend (here do not fork straight onto the ascending trail). Immediately after the bend a short-cut can be taken to the left along a washed-out trail – however, we remain on the track that loops around to a valley notch (in the valley floor a path forks right to Jardín de Las Creces, →Walk 18) and soon afterwards narrows to a footpath leading through vineyards. After a few minutes the path broadens again into a road continuing into the valley to reach the man-made lake Arure and the main street (Acardece district). Descend along this in not quite 10 min to the village centre of **Arure**, 826 m, with the bar »Concita« (bus stop for lines 1 and 6).

Remain another 5 min along the main street then, in the sharp left-hand bend, turn right onto the street towards the Ermita El Santo to follow this always straight on (after 100 m ignore a right fork to Mirador del Santo; the street becomes a track at the end). About 25 min later, shortly after a road forks to the right leading to a rubbish tip, bear right onto a cobblestone trail and in about 20 min pass the highest point of the plateau **La Mérica**, 857 m (survey post). Enjoying a breath-taking view of La Palma and El Hierro in the distance and Gomera's highest peaks, continue a steady descent along the gently-sloped tableland. Directly before the zigzag descent to La Calera, consider a possible detour to the sheer cliff's edge Riscos de la Mérica (10 min one-way; glorious downward view of La Playa and Playa del Inglés). Now with constant views of the Valle Gran Rey descend to **La Calera**. Here turn right along the village street then over a stepped trail return to the main road.

31 From Arure to Taguluche

Splendid panoramic circuit route in the »palm valley« of Taguluche

Arure – Ermita del Santo – Taguluche – Puerto – Taguluche – Arure

Starting point: Lower village limits of Arure, 826 m (bus stop for lines 1, 6).

Walking time: Arure – Taguluche (turn-about at the street's end) 1½ hrs, excursion to boat's landing 1 hr, Taguluche – Arure 2 hrs; total time 4½ hrs.

Ascent: 850 m.

Grade: Strenuous circuit route via a sometimes steep, sometimes fairly precipitous trail which requires sure-footedness.

Refreshment: Bar/restaurants in Arure.

Combination possible with Walks 29/30, 32 and 33.

During the descent to the secluded village Taguluche enjoy phenomenal panoramic views of the Galión Mountains and of the palm-dotted high valley – a marvellous trail, leading through pine forests and terraces to descend to the steep coastline. The return route along the opposite flank of the valley is just as unforgettable.

In the hairpin bend at the lower village limits of **Arure**, a street to the Ermita El Santo forks away (sign). After a good 100 m along this, fork to the right onto a cobblestone trail. This passes under an aqueduct then reaches the **Mirador del Santo** (restaurant), one of the most commanding overlooks on the island. 50 m after the chapel bear left at a fork (straight on leads to Alojera, →Walk 33) and continue along the narrow trail in long bends sometimes over steep steps. Soon leave the sunny pine wood behind then some minutes later, the trail forks again. Remain on the descending trail that is at first somewhat overgrown then continue the climb down along the left edge of a scrub wood, parallel to a power line. Soon after, the *camino* becomes a track that soon merges into an intersecting track. Straight on a path continues that soon merges into a street. Descend along this for about 100 m until a broad trail forks to the left then passes a transformer station on the mountain ridge and at the end descends over steps through vegetable and fruit gardens. Finally reach the village street of **Taguluche**, 200 m (10 min to the right, at the second fork in the street bearing left, reach the Ermita San Salvador, where you can connect up with Walk 32) and follow this to the left for a few minutes descending to the turnabout at the street's end.

A stepped trail continues straight on and immediately becomes a cobblestone trail. A quarter hour later pass immediately to the right of the last large

Descent through the palm-dotted mountain valley of Taguluche.

group of houses. Now the trail descends to the right through reeds and rushes into the Barranco de Taguluche but remains to the left of the stream. Not until a few minutes later does the trail cross over the stream bed to lead bearing right (at the end very narrow and precipitous) in 10 min to the former **boat landing** (½ hr from the turnabout) – a lovely spot – unfortunately a bit rough for a dip in the sea – with views of the sheer cliff walls of La Mérica and of the Galión Mountains.

Back at the turnabout, return a few metres along the street then turn right onto the concrete, stepped trail and continue straight ahead on the *camino*. 50 m on, just after the last house, turn left onto a faint path ascending in zig-zags that soon crosses over a water conduit and continues climbing in a steady traverse along the slope. After half an hour, change over to the left flank of the *barranco* to continue the climb through a palm grove (after 100 m ignore a left fork!). Steady on along the often stone-paved and cairn-marked main trail that, 25 min after crossing the *barranco*, begins a traverse to the right and, over stretches of beige-coloured outcrops, crosses over to a gentle valley gap bordered to the left by reddish »crags« and marked by pine trees. From here swing in a steep ascent to the crest of the ridge. After another 10 strenuous min of climbing, reach a road. Here, turn left to return to **Arure** (a right turn leads to a descent via La Mérica to La Calera, →Walks 29/30).

32 From Taguluche into the Galión Mountains

Circuit route in a remote massif populated by herds of goats

Taguluche – Barranco de Guarañel – Galión – Taguluche

Starting point: Ermita San Salvador in Taguluche, 200 m (no bus service; via the road from Chorros de Epina or by foot in 1½ hrs from Arure, →Walk 31).

Walking time: Taguluche – the saddle close to the Alojera road 1¼ hrs, excursion to the Galión Mountains not quite 1 hr, saddle – Taguluche 1¼ hrs; total time 3½ hrs.

Ascent: About 500 m.

Grade: Strenuous circuit route via a sometimes narrow, sometimes quite precipitous path. In summer very hot.

Alternative: Descent to Playa de Guariñén (a good ½ hr): from the church square you can already see a street that continues a descent to the sea. This forks away from the village street 30 m after the street leading to the church and ends after not quite 2 km at a turnabout. From here continue along a narrow *camino* descending in 10 min to the small gravel beach.

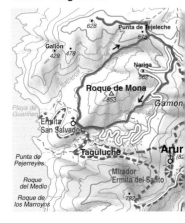

Combination possible with Walks 33 and 31 (→Walk 33, Alternatives).

This peaceful circuit route leads along a narrow goat path – the only approach to the centre of the untamed Galión Mountains: a bold rocky massif reaching a good 600 m that offers adventurous rambles.

About 1 km before the end of the street in **Taguluche** and in a sharp left-hand bend, a street forks away to the right leading over to the Ermita San Salvador. About 20 m before the street ends next to the chapel, an indistinct path forks to the right in a short ascent then traverses the slope along the foot of the Roque de Mona. The path is somewhat narrow and exposed sometimes, but not really precipitous. In an up-and-down walk, pass a small, deeply-cut gully and after not quite half an hour finally reach the floor of the **Barranco de Guarañel** then cross over this. The cairn-marked trail now ascends to the right to a mountain ridge then continues climbing to the right of a drawn-out basalt wall to finally reach a **saddle** (fork).

If you prefer to skip the actually very short, but rather unpleasantly precipitous path that leads into the Galión Mountains, turn right to reach the nearby road to Alojera / Chorros de Epina. We turn left onto the distinct path that traverses the slope and after a few minutes reaches a small open plateau with a view of Alojera. Here it is best to leave the slope path which becomes

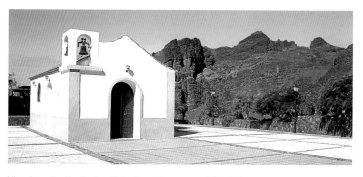

View from the Ermita San Salvador to the untamed Galión Mountains.

increasingly precipitous to instead ascend at first to the right along the mountain ridge, then bearing left towards a clearly visible path that ascends from Alojera. Climb this path to the left to reach a notch with a pasture gate (20 min from the saddle) then turn to the path ascending to the right. This leads in a few minutes to a sparse mountain meadow in front of a prominent towering crag at the upper edge of which we can enjoy a breathtaking view of Alojera as well as Tazo and possibly the neighbouring island of La Palma. If your heart is still pumping with wanderlust continue along the traces of path into the craggy wilderness of the **Galión Mountains** (10 min later reach a notch with a downward view of the sea); also at the pasture gate along the path to the left you can venture to other lovely overlooks.

Back at the saddle, follow the trail to the road nearby (a good 5 min) then turn to the left for a short way onto a *camino* ascending to the right. This forks after a few minutes about 100 m in front of a power pylon. Here bear to the right (to the left past the power pylon you can reach Arure). The somewhat washed-out trail leads in a lightly descending traverse along the slope and then some minutes later meets the road to Taguluche at a hairpin bend. Continue the ascent on the other side of the road to reach the **cemetery** of Taguluche. At the cemetery gate turn left passing a power pylon onto a lovely but ill-maintained *camino*. This descends into a *barranco* and crosses over to the other side reaching a palm grove. Shortly after, by the next power pylon, reach a covered water channel. Continue left along the main trail at the edge of the palm grove then, near a stone house, pass below to the left of a larger water reservoir. Finally reach a broad road to continue along this until meeting a descending path at the edge of a belt of rushes and palm trees to reach the nearby street. Here right, and in the sharp left-hand bend bear right to return in a good 10 min to the Ermita San Salvador in **Taguluche**.

33 From Arure to Alojera

Panoramic mountain trail with a descent into the Alojera Valley

Arure – Ermita del Santo – Alojera and back

Starting point: The lower village limits of Arure, 826 m (bus stop for lines 1, 6).
Walking time: Arure – road to Taguluche not quite 1¼ hrs, road – Alojera ¾ hr, return a good 2 hrs; total time 4 hrs.
Ascent: A good 600 m.
Grade: Strenuous walk along a some-times steep and precipitous trail requiring sure-footedness.
Refreshment: Bars in Arure and Alojera.
Alternatives: Circuit route (for physically fit hikers): from the road to Taguluche via Walk 32 to Taguluche and from there returning via Walk 31 to Arure (including the excursion to Alojera a total of 6 hrs). – From Alojera to the bar/restaurant Chorros de Epina (bus stop for line 4): pass to the left of the church square to descend to the asphalt road, leaving this 10 min later by turning right onto the track to Tazo (shortly after Cubaba you could take the old *camino* to the left to short-cut the broad bend in the track). From Tazo ascend the *camino* to the road that continues to Chorros de Epina (3 hrs from Alojera). Alternatively, you could ascend from Alojera to Chorros de Epina directly along a *camino* leading pretty much parallel to the road (1¾ hrs).
Tip: The Playa de Alojera, which can be reached via an access road from Alojera, is one of the island's best sand beaches. Also very lovely is the Playa del Trigo: climb down a path from the road between Alojera and Playa de Alojera at the fork in the sharp left-hand bend 700 m above Playa de Alojera; continue the descent always along the ridge above the coastline then descend to the right into the *barranco*, leaving this again 50 m to the right. Now a steep and exposed ascent to a plateau and from there climb down easily along the path to reach the beach; 20 min).

From the overlook platform next to the Ermita del Santo, a spectacular panoramic trail, although sometimes a little precipitous, leads along the sheer cliff towards Alojera and opens superb views of the Taguluche Valley and the Galión Mountains. The second leg of the route is not so nice, descending an unpleasant scree-slippery *camino* into the fertile Alojera Valley.
In the hairpin bend at the lower village limits of Arure a road branches off to-

The first stretch of the route leads through the steep slopes above the Taguluche Valley.

wards the Ermita El Santo (sign); leave this again a good 100 m on by turning right onto a cobblestone trail. This leads under an aqueduct and after a few minutes reaches the **Mirador del Santo** (restaurant), with a lovely downward view of Taguluche's valley basin.

50 m after the chapel remain on the trail continuing straight on (the *camino* forking left leads to Taguluche , →Walk 31). Now an unforgettable, sometimes exposed, mountain hike begins along the almost sheer cliff wall – pine trees provide a bit of shade now and again. After 20 min pass a spring (goat trough). Now a short zigzagging descent then the route continues in a pleasant traverse. In easy up-and-down walking, the *camino* passes along a beautiful basalt cliff, crosses precipitous sandy gullies and then after three quarters of an hour finally reaches a mountain spur which presents a lovely view of the palm-studded Alojera Valley, criss-crossed with gullies from water erosion. Along the mountain ridge heading into the valley, the somewhat steep, scree-slippery trail descends to reach the road to Taguluche at a hairpin bend. On the other side (cairns) continue the climb down towards Alojera. After half an hour the scree-covered *camino* reaches a pretty valley gap with palm trees. Cross over this to the right then traverse past the first houses heading towards a transformer tower to reach a street. Descend along this for 10 min to reach the church square of **Alojera**, 260 m (telephone booth, bars, bus stop for line 4 on the main street).

The Northern Island

Vallehermoso, Agulo and Hermigua

Vallehermoso is the north-western island's main town.

The northern island falls completely under the influence of the trade winds: in contrast to the relatively barren south, the landscape here is dominated by wide, fertile valleys with picturesque palm groves and ever-verdant cultivated terraces as well as expansive forests. The abundance of water and the excesses of Nature pay a certain price, however: the northern half is frequently shrouded in clouds, sometimes even plagued with rain, while in the south, perfect beach weather rules the day.

Vallehermoso, north-western Gomera's main town, is situated directly at the foot of the mighty Roque El Cano reigning over the valley. Here is also the meeting point for numerous heavenly valleys blessed with palm groves and cultivated terraces; these join up with the Barranco del Valle to complete their journey to the sea. Bordering to the east, the relatively barren Tamargada Valley still boasts the ancient, typically Canarian »long houses«. Tamargada and Simancas take the prize as the best-preserved villages in traditional Canarian style. Passing through Las Rosas you will finally come to **Agulo**. This picturesque village owes much of its charm to a maze of narrow cobblestone passageways and quaint houses with wooden balconies. Agulo's reputation as the most beautiful village on Gomera, if not the most beautiful of the Canary Islands, also owes much to an exceptionally pictorial setting: the valley basin above the steep coastline is surrounded by dramatic cliff walls and also presents a stupendous view of Teide on the neighbouring island of Tenerife. Driving along the Carretera del Norte and shortly after Agulo reach the long, drawn-out **Hermigua** Valley. This is the valley on La Gomera boasting the greatest abundance of water; at the valley bottom, an intensive cultivation of bananas is in operation. The natural landmarks of the community, whose main village is situated in the lower part of the Barranco de Monteforte, are the twin crags of San Pedro. The Río Cedro, the only stream on Gomera that flows year-round, also converges here. Not far from Hermigua, holiday-makers can enjoy the only northern beach worth mentioning – the Playa de La Caleta.

The Hermigua Valley is characterised by the steeply towering, fantastically jagged Cumbre Carbonera as well as the Enchereda chain extending to the east of this – both areas are unique natural pockets, for the most part still unspoilt. This is also true of the greater part of the Bosque del Cedro (although named after the juniper cedar, this tree has become a rarity here), established and protected as a national park since 1981. The picturesque village of El Cedro lies in the heart of the park, and is the ideal starting point for excursions into the fascinating laurisilva forest.

STARTING POINTS FOR WALKS

Chorros de Epina, 830 m

Picnic place and day-tripper's restaurant on the Vallehermoso – Valle Gran Rey road (bus stop for line 4). Walking trails to the west coast, the north-west tip of the island, Vallehermoso and in the Parque Nacional de Garajonay.

Vallehermoso, 186 m

The north-west's main town (bus stop for lines 3, 4, 5 and 7) offers numerous walking opportunities – for example through the southern tributary valleys, to Las Rosas, Tamargada and Chorros de Epina.

Hermigua, 103 m

The north-east's main town (bus stop for lines 3 and 5) offers numerous walking opportunities – for example to El Cedro, Cumbre Carbonera and also Tagaluche.

El Cedro, 850 m

A little village in the heart of the Bosque del Cedro (next bus stop at Cruce de la Zarcita for line 1). Walking trails to Hermigua, Meríga and Alto del Contadero.

Alto del Contadero, 1350 m

Car park on the mountain road, 1.2 km north of the junction at Pajarito (here the next bus stop for line 1). Walking trails to Laguna Grande, Hermigua and Garajonay.

Laguna Grande, 1250 m

Picnic place and day-tripper's restaurant on the mountain road, across from the turn-off of the road to Las Rosas (no bus service). Walking trails to El Cercado and Garajonay.

Centro de Visitantes Juego de Bolas, 750 m

National Park Visitor Centre on the road between Las Rosas and Laguna Grande (no bus service). Walking trails to Vallehermoso, Las Rosas, Agulo, Hermigua and in the Parque Nacional de Garajonay.

34 From Vallehermoso to Chorros de Epina

Pleasant but long circuit route above the Vallehermoso Valley

Vallehermoso – Montaña Blanca – Chorros de Epina – Pista forestal La Meseta – Presa de los Gallos – Los Loros – Vallehermoso

Starting point: Plaza de la Constitución in Vallehermoso, 186 m (bus stop for lines 3, 4, 5, 7).
Walking time: Vallehermoso – Chorros de Epina 2 hrs, Chorros de Epina – start of the Pista forestal La Meseta ¼ hr, Pista forestal La Meseta – Presa de los Gallos 1½ hrs, Presa de los Gallos – Vallehermoso 1¼ hrs; total time 5 hrs.
Ascent: 650 m.

Grade: The circuit route requires perseverance, but can otherwise be described as easy (long stretches over roads and tracks).
Refreshment: Bar/restaurants in Vallehermoso and at Chorros de Epina.
Alternative: Starting or ending at Chorros de Epina (bus stop for line 4).
Combination possible with Walks 22 and 35.

Ascent to Montaña Blanca – backwards view of Vallehermoso with the Roque El Cano.

Get acquainted with the marvellous Vallehermoso Valley via this long circuit route: the ascent to the day-tripper restaurant Chorros de Epina passes over the bleak and barren slopes of the Montaña Blanca, while the pleasant middle stretch leads along a forestry track at the edge of an ever-verdant laurel wood; finally, the return route crosses through an idyllic palm valley.

From the *plaza* in **Vallehermoso** ascend via the Calle Mayor passing between the Caja Canarias and the bar »Central«. After 100 m, pass house number 21 then turn left onto the stepped trail. A bit higher, cross over the main road then continue the climb to the left (at the fork a few minutes later bear left). Next to the last house, the stepped trail becomes a broad *camino*. This leads along a mountain ridge towards a transmission station high above us while frequently changing sides along the ridgeline. During the pleasant climb up enjoy a commanding overview of the Vallehermoso Valley especially from a rocky ledge which we reach in an hour to the left of the trail. The scrub wood gradually thickens and giant cactus trees appear at the trail's edge. After a total of 1¾ hrs, traverse below the transmitter then meet up with an asphalt road; here left, and at the fork 10 min later straight on, descending to the main road Vallehermoso – Valle Gran Rey. Follow this shortly to the right to the nicely-situated day-tripper's restaurant **Chorros de Epina**, 830 m (bus stop for line 4). From here, we recommend the short excursion to the Epina Springs: just after the restaurant, directly in front of

Downwards view of Epina from Chorros de Epina.

the national park sign, a road forks to the right and after a few minutes ends at a picnic place by the Ermita San Isidro – to the right below the chapel are springs reported to possess healing properties.

Return on the main road heading towards Vallehermoso then after a good quarter hour turn right onto the »Camino forestal La Meseta« (sign). The broad forestry track leads in easy up-and-down walking at about 700 m in altitude at the edge of the national park offering a splendid panoramic view of the Vallehermoso Valley – some stretches also pass through shady valley gaps with towering laurel trees. After an hour along the track reach a mountain ridge where a distinct path crosses over our track (→Walk 22). 20 min later reach the man-made lake **Presa de los Gallos**, 680 m – here the track ends.

To the left, a scree-covered path continues, leading along a conduit at the floor of the Barranco de la Cuesta to reach a broad road after a good quarter hour. Turn left onto this to **Los Loros**, 500 m, then continue the route along the seldom-used asphalt road that begins here. This leads through one of the island's most picturesque valleys, passing the Encantadora lake after a half hour. Another half hour later reach the bar/restaurant »Garajonay« at the village limits of **Vallehermoso**. Here turn left onto the shopping street to return to the *plaza*.

On the return route, the Roque El Cano comes into view, reigning over the valley.

35 From Vallehermoso to Cumbre de Chigueré

Circuit route to the sensational overlooks on the island's north-west tip

Vallehermoso – Teselinde – Ermita de Santa Clara – Cumbre de Chiguerés – Ermita de la Virgen de Guadalupe – Chiguerés – Buenavista – Playa de Vallehermoso – Vallehermoso

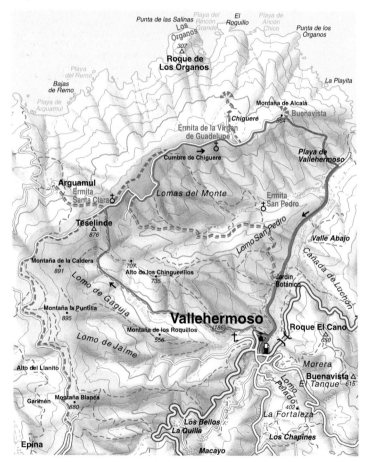

Starting point: Plaza de la Constitución in Vallehermoso, 186 m (bus stop for lines 3, 4, 5, 7).

Walking time: Vallehermoso – Ermita de Santa Clara 1½ hrs, Ermita de Santa Clara – Ermita de la Virgen de Guadalupe ½ hr, Ermita de la Virgen de Guadalupe – Buenavista 10 min, Buenavista – Playa de Vallehermoso 1 hr, Playa de Valle-hermoso – Vallehermoso ¾ hr; total time 4 hrs (excursion via Chigueré to the Los Órganos view, add ½ hr).

Ascent: 600 m.

Grade: Although an exhausting circuit route, generally pleasant when not count-ing the somewhat steep, bumpy descent to Playa de Vallehermoso.

Refreshment: Bar/restaurants in Vallehermoso, kiosk on the Playa de Vallehermoso.

Alternatives: If you prefer a pleasant track route without much ascent and descent, take the track from Chorros de Epina to Ermita de Santa Clara and continue to Buenavista (4 hrs there and back). – If you prefer to shorten the walk, just after the Ermita de Santa Clara turn right onto the (at first) broad trail to return to Valle-hermoso (a good hour shorter).

Combination possible with Walk 34.

Despite the considerable difference in elevation between the start and the destination, the circuit route to Cumbre de Chigueré belongs to one of the most pleasant described in this guide. A well-maintained, old *camino* pro-vides the way, ascending from Vallehermoso to the Teselinde massif. After-wards, a pleasant high mountain ramble follows along the Cumbre, open-ing marvellous views over the north-west tip of the island – especially note-worthy is that of the Roque de los Órganos. The climax of the tour is, how-ever, the descent to Playa de Vallehermoso presenting astounding views of the steep northern coastline as well as the Vallehermoso Valley. Unfortu-nately, the return along the road to Vallehermoso, although traffic is fairly sparse, is a bit of a bitter pill to swallow.

From the *plaza* in **Vallehermoso** ascend along the Calle Mayor which leads between the Caja Canarias and the bar »Central«. After a few minutes next to house number 38 directly above the church, turn left onto a stepped trail that soon meets the main road to Valle Gran Rey. Turn right here and then leave the road behind again in the next right-hand bend (Guardia Civil build-ing) by forking left onto the little street that leads straight on to the cemetery. To the right of the cemetery, a lovely *camino* continues which crosses the *barranco* over a little bridge then forks immediately after. Here, continue along the right fork passing a few houses and terraces then ascend into the valley of the Barranco de la Era Nueva. After a good half hour of walking, pass a solitary stone house then a bit later a large reservoir. Shortly thereaf-ter the trail forks. Ignore the trail forking left to the *barranco* floor then a few minutes later cross over an old circular threshing yard. The *camino* ascends for a while along the *barranco* floor then begins a traverse along the left-hand slope. For some minutes follow along a water conduit then immedi-ately after, the trail leads between a stone wall more than two metres high and a patch of rushes and reeds then continues bearing right further into the valley. Gradually leave the last palm trees behind and climb up the right

During the high ramble on the Cumbre de Chiguaré; here next to the Ermita de la Virgen de Guadalupe – relish a stupendous view of Tenerife.

flank of the valley through scrub wood, later passing eucalyptus trees to reach the crest of the ridge. The trail forks here – a sharp turn to the right offers an excursion to the highest point of the ridgeline where you can enjoy a lovely bird's-eye view of Vallehermoso and its tributary valleys (¼ hr one way; distinct path). We turn left to continue along the broad main trail, still ascending the ridge for a short stretch (ignore the path descending to the right) and after a traverse through the Teselinde east slope finally reach (about 10 min total time) the **Ermita de Santa Clara**, 735 m, where the trail merges into a broad track road. From the chapel (built in 1888) enjoy a superlative view of the neighbouring island of La Palma as well as the hamlet of Arguamul.

By the chapel, a decision must be made: whether to continue on the panoramic but unfortunately arduous path along the ridgeline or to take the track passing to the right of the chapel. We take the second choice by continuing along below the ridgeline enjoying a more-and-more sweeping view of Tenerife. After 25 min at an ochre-coloured landscape sculptured by erosion meet up again with the ridgeline of the Cumbre de Chiguaré (the ridgeline trail merges from the left) and reach a lovely spot to take a break with a choice of rocky perches. In front of us, we can already see the **Ermita de la Virgen de Guadalupe**, 640 m, which we reach 5 min later.

After another 5 min a road forks to the left. This offers a short excursion to the abandoned hamlet of **Chiguaré**, 570 m. From here, not to miss the staggering downward view of the Roque de los Órganos, clamber over the rock wall next to the highest house, descend bearing a bit to the right then follow the sometimes green-marked path through overgrown terraces until reaching a large cairn on the next mountain ridge – the renowned »organ pipes« Los Órganos are unfortunately not visible from this point, this pleasure is reserved to boat excursionists (under no circumstances attempt a descent along the steep slope towards Roque de los Órganos – this is extremely dangerous and foolhardy!).

Returning to the track, it is only another 10 min to reach the end of the track road at **Buenavista**, 564 m – from this overlook enjoy an incomparable view sweeping the steep coastline of the island's north-west tip, over the Vallehermoso Valley with the Roque El Cano as well as all the way to Tenerife.

In the depression directly in front of the Buenavista a distinct trail forks away from the track near a large cairn. This traverses the slope towards the north-east, crossing a miniature pine wood at the same time. At the end, the trail continues descending along a mountain ridge heading toward the Playa de Vallehermoso, however leave this behind half an hour later by bearing right to cross over to the next barely distinguishable mountain ridge. Along this, the bumpy *camino* continues the climb down and after 20 min bears right towards a gentle valley notch through which, passing rubbish and a few houses, we descend to the road in the Barranco del Valle. To the left it is only a few minutes to **Playa de Vallehermoso**, where a rest area has been established – to the right, the road leads straight on through the valley with banana plantations to return to the *plaza* of **Vallehermoso** (half-way along: the Jardín Botánico del Descubrimiento).

The Roque de los Órganos from nearby Chigueré.

36 From Vallehermoso to El Tión

Unforgettably scenic circuit route at the foot of the mighty Roque El Cano

Vallehermoso – El Tión – Roque El Cano – Vallehermoso

Starting point: Plaza de la Constitución in Vallehermoso, 186 m (bus stop for lines 3, 4, 5, 7).
Walking time: Vallehermoso – El Tión 1¼ hrs, El Tión – asphalt street near Rosa de las Piedras ¾ hr, asphalt street – Roque El Cano 1 hr, Roque El Cano – Vallehermoso ½ hr; total time 3½ hrs.
Ascent: 600 m.

Grade: Mostly easy circuit walk with only a few somewhat steeper stretches.
Refreshment: Bar/*bodegon* »Roque Blanco« near Rosa de las Piedras; bar/restaurants in Vallehermoso.
Alternative: From El Tión a possible descent via the Roque Blanco and the Embalse La Encantadora to Vallehermoso (1½ hrs).

Vallehermoso offers nature-lovers an abundance of walking trails that connect with tributary valleys and the nearby mountain crests. This circuit route is especially unforgettable leading through the hamlet of El Tión to the foot of the Roque El Cano which reigns over the valley.
From the *plaza* in **Vallehermoso** descend along the main road toward Hermigua and after the big playground turn right onto the ascending street (direction »Garabato«), from now on always following this straight on (after ¼ hr, the street is no longer asphalt). This leads through one of the many idyllic tributary valleys that are so typical for the environs of Vallehermoso: delightful cultivated terraces, palm groves and scattered hamlets characterise the fertile valley. After three quarters hour of walking, the narrow road enters a scrub wood. Before us, we can already see the dam wall of the Embalse de Vallehermoso, as well as the hamlet El Tión – the final destination of the first leg of the route, perched on the hang above and to the right. Now, after a sharp left-hand bend, pass directly above a waterworks. About 30 m past the waterworks and 250 m before the dam wall, a distinct, old *camino* forks sharply to the right and begins a winding ascent over a steep

mountain ridge to **El Tión**, 600 m. After 25 min of climbing reach the first house of the delightfully-situated hamlet, then the trail forks immediately after.

Bear left at the fork passing through terraces (the trail to the right heads towards the Embalse La Encantadora) and a few minutes later next to a power pylon ascend steeply to the right along a track ending here. This climbs in not quite half an hour to reach a plateau at about 750 m in altitude near the hamlet of Rosa de las Piedras.

On the plateau, bear to the left passing an overlook platform to follow the street passing below and to the right of the **restaurant »Roque Blanco«**. About 250 m on (5 min; immediately after to the right of the street – the Campamiento Garabato) fork away from the road to Las Rosas onto a descending road to the left that passes a shrine after some minutes and 100 m after this reaches a saddle and a gate. In front of this continue to the left along a lightly descending *camino*. This very fine mountain trail, although sometimes a bit overgrown, bears to the left below the ridgeline of the mountain ridge descending towards Vallehermoso offering fabulous views over the valleys to the south of Vallehermoso – after a quarter hour, the dramatic Roque El Cano and Vallehermoso also appear. The *camino* leads for a while along the slope then follows the narrow ridge and descends to a saddle located at the foot of the cliff wall of the **Roque El Cano**, 650 m.

Enjoying a superlative view of the north-west island's main town, descend now to the left along the broad *camino* to reach the street; here turn right to return in 10 min to the *plaza* of **Vallehermoso**.

Climbing down from Roque El Cano to Vallehermoso.

37 From Agulo to the Centro de Visitantes Juego de Bolas

Spectacular circuit route with a climb along the sheer cliff wall above Agulo

Agulo – Mirador de Agulo – La Palmita – Juego de Bolas – Cañada Grande – Agulo

Starting point: Agulo, 190 m (bus stop for lines 3, 5).
Walking time: Agulo – Mirador de Agulo ¾ hr, Mirador de Agulo – La Palmita 1 hr, La Palmita – Juego de Bolas 20 min, Juego de Bolas – Agulo 2 hrs; total time 4 hrs.
Ascent: 600 m.
Grade: The ascent along the sheer cliff wall above Agulo requires sure-footedness and an excellent head for heights but is not truly exposed. Also, the return route

from the National Park Visitor Centre is sometimes somewhat steep.
Refreshment: Bar/restaurants in Agulo and a bar/restaurant next to the National Park Visitor Centre (closed Mondays).
Combination possible with Walk 38 from Agulo or starting at the fork in the trail during the return to Agulo.
Notice: The National Park Visitor Centre is open daily from 9:30 a.m. until 4:30 p.m. (closed Mondays).

Agulo is not only the prettiest village on the island, but also boasts the starting point for one of the island's most spectacular walking routes: this winds through the middle of the dramatic, reddish sheer cliff wall ascending to the Mirador de Agulo, one of Gomera's most ostentatious overlooks, then continues through a high mountain valley to La Palmita. From there, it is only a

Agulo – one of the most delightful of the island's villages.

stone's throw to the National Park Visitor Centre »Juego de Bolas« that is well worth a stopover. The return route follows an equally lovely track leading above the Barranco de las Rosas.

The starting point for the walk is the bus stop on the Carretera del Norte in **Agulo** (plenty of parking). Passing the school, ascend along the main road to Casa Aixa. Just to the left of this, a stepped trail ascends passing through terraces and after a few minutes (right) crosses over a cobblestone street then the main road in another 5 min. On the other side (sign »La Palmita«) begin a steep climb heading in a straight line to the foot of the sheer cliff to reach this 10 min later. Without missing a beat, continue the climb in zig-zags through the rocks. 10 min later the ingeniously-constructed trail passes a eucalyptus tree, then another soon after. Finally, after a total of 40 min, reach one of Gomera's most beautiful overlooks – the **Mirador de Agulo**, 425 m (stone column), presenting one of the island's most photo-qraphed motifs: the picturesque village of Agulo, surrounded by banana plantations and terraces as well as framed by sheer cliff walls; in the distance, Tenerife's majestic Teide provides the backdrop. To the right, after heavy rainfall, a mighty waterfall tumbles over the sheer cliff wall.

Now the trail continues into the valley, soon ascending and bearing to the right, leading above and past the dam wall of the **Embalse de Agulo**. Soon after, meet a track and now ascend always along this into the valley (after a

The La Palmita's chapel in festive attire.

few minutes, above the holiday resort, left). A quarter hour past the man-made lake, the track changes over to the left flank then 10 min later returns again to the right flank of the valley. Directly in front of us and perched on a mountain ridge, we can already see the chapel at La Palmita. Not quite 10 min after changing valley flanks and about 100 m after passing a turn-about to the right of the cobblestone street, a trail forks to the right (do not take the first, but instead take the second trail). This ascends in 5 min to the Ermita San Isidro in **La Palmita**, 700 m, and a picnic place (you can also reach this via the cobblestone street then right onto the street leading here). Now follow the street to the right to reach the Centro de Visitantes **Juego de Bolas**, 750 m (National Park Visitor Centre, 20 min). Here you can gain an interesting insight into the island's geology as well as the flora and fauna; workshops present the handicrafts typical to La Gomera.

Pass the visitor centre to the right to continue along an asphalt street that forks 150 m on. Here bear left onto the more red-coloured road, shortly ascending and then lightly descending in a traverse through the slope of the Cañada Grande. After a good quarter hour the panoramic trail leads past and below a little pine wood. Here bear left at the fork to enter a reddish landscape marked by erosion, to bear slightly left away from the road following along an eroded gully (watch out for cairns; to the left of the gully, a tall solitary eucalyptus tree!) descending in a northerly direction. Cross for some metres through a grey-coloured zone of erosion then continue the climb down along a cobblestone *camino* while enjoying a view of the Barranco de las Rosas. Three quarters hour after Juego de Bolas, the trail forks near a group of pines. Turn right here to continue above the farmstead (the left fork is a trail to Las Rosas, →Walk 38) descending along a broad *camino* towards the sea to finally reach the Carretera del Norte after another three quarters hour of walking. Follow this 100 m to the right then 25 m before the Túnel de Agulo turn left again onto the old *camino* following this straight on, passing a projecting rock then reaching the cemetery at **Agulo** (to the left a possible excursion to Playa de San Marcos). From here, a cobblestone street continues into the village with its typical Canarian passageways. Always head straight on, past the church square to return to the main road.

The return route leads through the slope above the Barranco de las Rosas.

38 From Hermigua to Vallehermoso

Wondrous walk above the north coast – but not without its seamy sides!

Playa de Hermigua – Lepe – Agulo – Las Rosas – Simancas – Tamargada – Vallehermoso

Starting point: Fork of the access road to Playa de Hermigua at the lower village limits of Hermigua, 70 m (bus stop for lines 3 and 5).

Destination: Plaza de la Constitución in Vallehermoso, 186 m (bus stop for lines 3, 4, 5, 7).

Walking time: Hermigua (fork to Playa de Hermigua) – Lepe 20 min, Lepe – Agulo ½ hr, Agulo – Las Rosas 1¾ hrs, Las Rosas – Simancas 1 hr, Simancas – Tamargada ½ hr, Tamargada – Vallehermoso 1½ hrs; total time 5½ hrs.

Ascent: A total of about 1000 m and 900 m in descent.

Grade: A long strenuous one-way tour that leads in constant up-and-down hiking above the north coast and requires physical fitness. The trail is very well-maintained except for the stretch between Tamargada and Vallehermoso; short stretches of the route are along the

Carretera del Norte.

Refreshment: Bar/restaurants in Playa de Hermigua, Agulo, Las Rosas and Vallehermoso.

Alternatives: The route can also begin or end in Agulo, Las Rosas or near Tamargada (all with bus stops for the lines 3 and 5 on the Carretera del Norte). – From Las Rosas, you could also take an asphalt road passing the Embalse de Amalhuigue to ascend towards Rosa de las Piedras then after a good ½ hr shortly after the Casas de Ambrosío, right along the trail from Walk 36 in 1½ hrs to descend to Vallehermoso. – From the Ermita in Tamargada, a possible descent to Playa de Tamargada (about 1 hr one-way).

Combination possible with Walk 37 from Agulo or from the fork in the trail along the continued route to Las Rosas.

This connecting route between Hermigua and Vallehermoso, although rich in diversity, is admittedly arduous, but the hiker will be rewarded with incomparable impressions of the island's north – the walk leads usually high above the northern coast touching Lepe, Agulo and Tamargada (probably the best-preserved and most original of the Canarian settlements), certainly three of Gomera's prettiest villages. Nevertheless, it is useless to hide the fact that the route also has a seamy side: especially the last stretch between Tamargada and Vallehermoso is choked with overgrowth and ill-maintained, on top of that, there is no way to avoid using the Carretera del Norte to continue on.

A sign marking the fork in the road from the Carretera del Norte onto the road to Playa de Hermigua can be found about 1 km below the lower village centre of **Hermigua**, 103 m, boasting a church. The access road leads in 10 min (at the bar »Piloto« to the left) to the stony **Playa de Hermigua** then again to the left in another 10 min to the hamlet of **Lepe**, 60 m, perched above the coast. At the end of the road, a stepped trail continues to the left ascending through terraces to reach the Carretera del Norte again (20 min). Follow this to the right for a good 5 min until reaching the village limits of **Agulo**, 190 m.

Next to the Café Bertermann turn right onto the village street then, immediately after passing the small store, take another right onto an intersecting street (Calle del Calvario) to follow this straight on to the church then further on to the cemetery on the other side of the village. It takes slightly less than a quarter hour to pass through this quaint settlement. Immediately after the cemetery, bear to the left along a broad ascending cobblestone trail. At a fork a few minutes later bear left and some minutes later at the Túnel de Agulo again reach the Carretera del Norte. Turn right and 50 m on, the broad *camino* continues to the left. This ascends steeply above the Barranco de las Rosas into the valley and after three quarters hour passes

directly above a farmstead. Here a *camino* forks left to the National Park Visitor Centre Juego de Bolas (→Walk 37) – however, we continue on the trail straight on (sign »Las Rosas«, a right fork 20 m later leads to a spring), continuing a pleasant mountain walk. 10 min later reach another fork. The main trail straight on is so overgrown and often slide-damaged that there is no other choice than to ascend to the left in steep bends to reach a farmstead (a good 5 min). At a stone wall 20 m above the farmstead meet an intersecting trail; turn right here and in 5 min ascend to a sandy mountain ridge. On the following mountain ridge (a copse of small eucalyptus trees) where we can already enjoy a lovely view of the high valley of Las Rosas, leave the trail to descend to the right without a trail over a sandy ridge (after 50 m, somewhat right along the eroded gully passing a power pylon; a property is to our left). Already after a few minutes reach a washed-out road, turning left onto this (the old, overgrown *camino* merges from the right). Passing the first houses of **Las Rosas**, 580 m, the now stone-paved road descends to a bridge then immediately after the bridge, descend to the right through the stream bed to reach the nearby Carretera del Norte. On the other side of the road, continue the descent along a path to the Barranco de las Rosas, cross the stream bed then 5 m above this, meet a trail that ascends to the left to the terraced vineyards above the stream bed. After a few minutes the now rocky trail climbs steeply to the right between terrace walls. This ascends in a straight line (25 m on, bear somewhat left) to the Carretera del Norte and merges with this to the right of the car park for the restaurant »Las Rosas«.

Follow the main road 30 m to the left and across from the telephone booth by the restaurant turn right onto a stepped trail which immediately after becomes a partially stone-paved *camino*. After a few minutes a trail turns right leading through the terraces and ascends to a group of houses (La Vega) on the crest of the ridge to meet a street there. On the other side, a *camino* continues, at first broad and stone-paved. This leads parallel to power pylons in an easy up-and-down traverse along the slope and after a good 10 min reaches the height of a mountain ridge. From here we can already see our next destination point: the villages of Simancas and Tamargada, as well as the Roque El Cano. The *camino* now bears to the right away from the power pylons and continues over the mountain ridge. Passing an old threshing yard and a few houses reach a washed-out road, following this for a few minutes only to leave it again at a sharp right-hand bend by continuing straight on a stony path that descends to the nearby Carretera del Norte. Follow this to the left for a good 10 min to reach a bus stop shelter. Turn right here onto the street to **Simancas**, 400 m, which descends in a quarter hour to the almost completely abandoned hamlet.

At the fork immediately above the palm tree-blessed *barranco* floor bear left onto the road that soon ends at a waterworks. 10 m before the waterworks, a small *camino* turns off to the right shortly descending then forking at a water conduit. Here turn left onto a pretty meadow trail that leads along the conduit ascending easily between terraced vineyards and, on the other side of the mountain ridge, descends just as easily to a fork shortly before reaching **Tamargada**, 400 m (not quite ½ hr from Simancas).

Bear right here and at the fork a few minutes later again to the right onto a broad, steeply descending cobblestone trail that changes over to the left valley flank some minutes later. Next to the Ermita de la Caridad del Cobre continue straight on the road then 100 m past the chapel continue straight on (not right). 25 m on, a trail forks to the right in front of a couple of houses. This descends along a water conduit and street lamps, ignoring a right-hand fork, to reach the Barranco de los Zarzales 5 min later then on the other side of the valley ascends steeply to a dirt road. Climb along this for 150 m then in a sharp left-hand bend again to the right onto an old *camino*. At the fork 25 m on, bear right once more. Now on a somewhat stony and overgrown trail leading straight on (shortly before the ridgeline, do not fork left) climb in 20 min to the crest of the ridge. The *camino* now descends in zigzags between *sabinas* with some stretches very overgrown while presenting a remarkable view of the Roque El Cano (after a good 10 min bear right at a fork) to reach the Barranco de la Culata, where after a good quarter hour we meet a pleasant intersecting trail and follow this down the valley. After 5 min this passes above a dam wall then changes over to the left flank of the valley shortly after. Passing between terraced vineyards reach the Barranco del Valle some minutes later and a fork in the trail – to the left, we can already see Vallehermoso. Bear left here (straight on). A few minutes later, the trail forks again. (If you bear right here onto a steep and narrow path, you could cross over to the other side of the valley through a stream bed of rushes and reeds then stoop through a small passage in a wall to enter the Jardín Botánico del Descubrimiento to pass through this and ascend to the main road). We continue by bearing left at the fork walking parallel to a large conduit. The trail dips down after 10 min – now following two conduits – gradually descending to the valley floor to reach this 5 min later. Pass a large water reservoir and follow the distinct path leading along the stream. Shortly after, change over to the right bank to meet an intersecting trail near a house; ascend along this to the right to reach the main road in not quite 10 min. Left along this then at the fork in the road shortly after, turn left to reach the *plaza* of **Vallehermoso** (not quite 10 min).

39 From Hermigua to Los Aceviños

Circuit walk to the waterfall at El Cedro and through the laurisilva forest

El Convento – Monteforte – Salto de Agua – El Cedro – Los Aceviños – Ermita de San Juán – El Convento

Starting point: El Convento, 250 m (bus stop for lines 3 and 5).
Walking time: Hermigua – El Cedro 1¾ hrs, El Cedro – Los Aceviños 1 hr, Los Aceviños – Ermita de San Juán a good 1¼ hrs, Ermita de San Juán – Hermigua ¾ hr; total time 5 hrs.
Ascent: A good 900 m.

Grade: Strenuous circuit route with steep ascents and descents. Sure-footedness required (especially when wet).
Refreshment: Bar/restaurants in Hermigua and in El Cedro, small store in Los Aceviños.
Combination possible with Walks 42 and 43.

This scenically impressive circuit tour with steep stretches of ascent and descent leads past the highest waterfall on the island to reach El Cedro. From there, circle back with a pleasant jaunt through the Bosque del Cedro. The return route follows a very panoramic trail presenting a marvellous overview of the Hermigua Valley.

The ascent leads through the untamed and idyllic Barranco de Monteforte; in the background – the twin crags »Los Gemelos«.

The starting point for the walk is the large church square below the Los Telares museum on the main street in **El Convento**, one of the highest districts of Hermigua. On the other side of the *plaza* a broad stepped trail steeply ascends through the village to reach a road (5 min). Take this to the right, passing below and between the steeply towering twin crags »Los Gemelos« to reach **Monteforte**, 350 m, in about a quarter hour.

Directly at the village limits, 30 m after the bar »Medina Los Roques«, a stepped trail with a green handrail turns to the left. Leave this again a few metres on by turning left onto a path following a water conduit. The tranquil trail leads up the valley passing between cultivated terraces. Next to a large water reservoir, the trail turns away from the conduit and then changes over to the left side of the valley. Subsequently, cross twice more over the Cedro Stream to reach a dam wall after an hour's walking time. Skirt around this to the right along the cobblestone trail. 100 m after the dam wall and shortly before a pretty cascade, the cobblestone trail bears right onto the slope, ascending steeply with a heavenly view of the Hermigua Valley and the island's highest waterfall. After a good half hour, by a high tension pylon, reach the valley head. Continue along the valley trail for about another 150 m then immediately after the La Vista campground, turn right onto the *camino Aceviños* towards the **bar/restaurant** »**La Vista**«. Already after a short ascent, pass the traditional bar/restaurant – or take a long relaxing break on the lovely restaurant terrace.

Behind the restaurant turn right onto a road ascending steeply. Not quite 5 min later, this forks at the same height as the Casa rural El Refugio – here continue climbing steeply straight on along the *camino*, now leaving the last houses of **El Cedro** behind. A few minutes later, the camino turns right to enter the laurel forest. After a good 10 min, ignore a path forking off to the left, then 5 min later, the trail merges into a forestry road. Follow this to the right for about 10 min until reaching a small group of houses located on a height; we can already make out Los Aceviños from here. Just after the

houses and immediately before a heather tree wood, turn left onto a washed-out trail at first descending along the edge of the scrub wood, then to the right and passing through it. After 10 min the trail forks at a large clearing (turn left here) then leads a few minutes later into a *barranco* with terraces. Change over to the other side of the valley then at a fork shortly after descend to the right to the valley floor, cross to the other side passing a high tension pylon then ascend to the right to reach an asphalt road.

The road leads left to the nearby hamlet of **Los Aceviños**, 900 m – but turn right here instead. Already a few minutes later, in the first right-

Shortly before the Ermita de San Juán; in the background – the Hermigua Valley.

hand bend, leave the road by forking off to the right onto a track which is asphalt-paved at first, crossing over the Barranco de Liria and then traversing the slope almost on the level. After a quarter hour when the track forks, bear to the left, then at another fork a few minutes later bear right, at yet another fork 5 min later again to the left. Immediately after reach a sharp right-hand bend with a terrific view of Tenerife. Here, a trail forks to the left, descending in a few minutes to a road. Continue the climb down along this and after a good 5 min savour a spectacular view of the Hermigua Valley with the Ermita de San Juán, of the Enchereda chain and all the way to Tenerife. Soon after, the *camino* hooks off to the right. Along this 5 min later pass a small overlook then the ruins of a house shortly after. In a sweeping bend, the *camino* now bears to the right to approach the rim of a valley notch, then left to a pine tree and descends steeply to cross the *barranco*. A quarter hour later reach the **Ermita de San Juán**, 400 m, with just about the entire Hermigua Valley spread out below – an eye-popping overlook!

If you wish, you can return along the access road to El Convento by turning right (1 hr). We follow the *camino*, that continues the steep descent, subsequently crossing two asphalt roads then, not quite half an hour later, reaches the Carretera del Norte in **Hermigua** next to the Museo Etnografico (bus stop shelter). Along this to the right return in not quite a quarter hour to the starting point of the walk.

31.1.07 · Great coastal walk – Tagaluche excursion not up to much! Good fish at playa del caleta.

40 From Hermigua to the Playa de La Caleta

To the steep coastline at the plunging cliffs of the Enchereda chain

Hermigua – Camiña – Casas del Palmar – Playa de La Caleta – Hermigua

Starting point: The church square at the lower village centre of Hermigua, 103 m (bus stop for lines 3 and 5).

Walking time: Hermigua – Camiña a good ¾ hr, Camiña – Casas del Palmar 1½ hrs, Casas del Palmar – Playa de La Caleta ¾ hr, Playa de La Caleta – Camiña a good ½ hr, Camiña – Hermigua a good ½ hr; total time 4¼ hrs.

Ascent: About 600 m.

Grade: Long but pleasant track route – the narrow, precipitous stretch between El Palmar and La Caleta requires a good head for heights.

Refreshment: Bar/restaurants in Hermigua, kiosk at the Playa de La Caleta.

Alternative: Walkers approaching by car can also begin the walk at the fork in the track at Camiña (1 hr shorter).

Tip: Bring along your bathing gear!

In front of the church in **Hermigua**, descend about 500 m along the main road, past the Casa Creativa then 20 m before the Cepsa petrol station turn right onto a broad, stepped trail. This descends into the Barranco de Monteforte, crosses over the stream bed and merges with an intersecting trail; take this to the right. Soon leave the *barranco* and its banana plantations behind to ascend over steps bearing left to reach the street on the other side of the valley. Now a choice must be made: easier and 15 min shorter is the ascent along the track (150 m to the right then turn left). Instead, we turn left to follow the street for a good 10 min until reaching the junction next to the road bridge. Here a stepped trail forks to the right (sign »Playa de La Caleta«), which we follow for 25 m only to leave it again by fork-

144

ing left onto a path. This climbs steeply (unpleasant when wet) and after a few minutes becomes a lovely *camino* presenting a fine view of the Playa de Hermigua below. After not quite half an hour reach the crest of the ridge (**Camiña**, 238 m) and a fork with two tracks.

If you want to descend to the Playa de La Caleta, turn left (15 m on, a *camino* to the right). We bear to the right onto the track road leading to the Casas del Palmar (sign) and during the pleasant ascent savour a superb view of Tenerife and the coast. Always following the main track heading straight on, reach another fork with two tracks 1¼ hours later: straight on (right) a forestry track continues to Enchereda (→Walk 2), but fork to the left instead and descend, passing a solitary farmstead, to the Casas del Palmar which have already come into view. 30 m after the first house a poorly-marked path forks left towards the ancient houses. It is easier, however to continue along the track. This leads in 10 min onto a mountain spur and forks there (straight on, a worth-while excursion to the secluded hamlet of **Tagaluche**, 200 m, situated in a magnificent valley basin at the foot of the Enchereda chain above the steep coastline). Take the sharp left fork and at the end of the road reach the ancient **Casas del Palmar**, 200 m.

Straight on, in the same direction as the road we have just left, a partially stone-paved path continues the route. This descends lightly traversing the slope (sensational field of blocky boulders), dipping down shortly some minutes later over a small mountain ridge then turns to the left towards the Barranco Cañada la Barraca only to leave it again somewhat above by turning sharply to the right. The path now ascends to a mountain spur then descends lightly along the slope above the coast (during this stretch, ignore the path forking right towards the Punta San Lorenzo – continue straight on). At the end descend to the left with a dizzying downward view of the Playa de La Caleta to reach the first terraces of La Caleta and meet an intersecting trail. Take this to the right to cross over to the track road (here asphalt), that returns again to Hermigua by turning left; we turn to the right and in 10 min reach the black sand beach **Playa de La Caleta**, where a picnic place and a *kiosco* present an ideal spot for a well-deserved break.

View from the trail to Playa de La Caleta.

41 Cumbre Carbonera

Short but interesting botanical climb to the »charcoal maker's« pass

Túnel de la Cumbre (La Carbonera) – Cumbre Carbonera and back

Location: Hermigua, 103 m.
Starting point: Bar/restaurant La Carbonera, 630 m, near km 13 on the Carretera del Norte – 200 m before the Túnel de la Cumbre (bus stop for lines 3, 5).
Walking time: Ascent not quite ¾ hr, descent a good ½ hr; total time 1¼ hrs.
Ascent: 250 m.
Grade: Steep stretches, but a short ascent along an overgrown, sometimes exposed *camino*, requiring sure-footedness.
Refreshment: Restaurant La Carbonera.
Alternatives: Begin the walk in Hermigua, El Convento: start off by ascend-

ing a good 1.5 km along the main road until reaching the sharp right-hand bend below the Embalse de Mulagua. Here turn left onto a track and 50 m on, next to a waterworks continue to the left along a trail then shortly after to the right ascending in zigzags until reaching a track that leads to the right to the Túnel de la Cumbre (1 hr, overgrown). – From the crest of the pass, a possible descent via Lomo Fragoso to San Sebastián (about 2½ hrs; note: the stretch along the south flank of the Cumbre Carbonera is sometimes slide-damaged and very overgrown!).

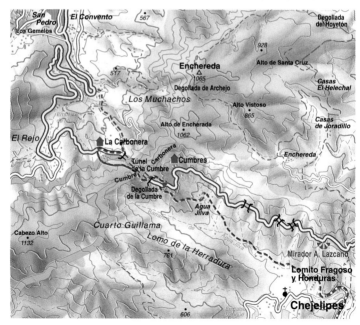

View from the bar/restaurant »La Carbonera« to the Cumbre.

The ancient, legendary *camino* crossing over the »charcoal-maker's pass« was formerly the most important connecting trail between the island capital and the Hermigua Valley. Unfortunately, nowadays it has fallen into rack and ruin – while the trail to the pass on the north side still remains in fair condition, on the south side entire stretches have been slide-damaged so that this leg of the route is only recommended to experienced mountain hikers. Despite this drawback, the short climb to the crest of the pass on the Cumbre Carbonera, although often shrouded in cloud, is absolutely worth the effort: the trail leads into one of the most fascinating laurisilva forests on the island, and from the top, you can enjoy a view sweeping over the Barranco de la Villa all the way to San Sebastián.

Across from the bar/restaurant »**La Carbonera**« the trail begins. The path climbs steeply at first but levels out later on (now some stretches are stone-paved) then bears left to continue climbing, passing above two houses. Soon after, a lovely view opens up over the Hermigua Valley. After a good ¼ hr reach a small gentle valley notch with a large block boulder where the continued route is difficult to discern – here pass to the left of the boulder ascending along the stream bed and 30 m on, to the right over stone steps to climb out of the valley notch. Now the continuing trail to the crest of the pass on the **Cumbre Carbonera**, 870 m (power pylon), is distinct once again – especially striking is the last stretch of trail through the mossy laurisilva forest with ferns up to 2 metres high, lichen-trimmed laurel trees and creeping blackberry bushes; along the trail's edge – even mushrooms can be found.

30.1.07 – too much water in tunnel – did circuit in reverse, mostly under trees on forest road.

42 El Cedro Roundabout

Forest circuit offering variety and a little athletic activity

Rejo road – El Cedro – Pista forestal a Los Aceviños y Meríga – Las Mimbreras – Pista forestal al Rejo – Montaña Quemada – Rejo road

Starting point: Lower hairpin bend, 800 m, of the road in the Rejo Valley – between the junction at El Rejo (Carretera del Norte) and the Cruce de la Zarcita (Carretera del Centro); parking possible. No bus service! Walkers dependent on public transportation best begin the route starting at Cruce de la Zarcita (bus stop for line 1): follow the street towards Hermigua for a good 1 km (20 min) then turn left on the street towards El Cedro (along this for about 10 min, reach the sharp bend at the foothills of the Montaña Quemada).

Walking time: Rejo road – El Cedro ¼ hr, El Cedro – Pista forestal a Los Aceviños y Meríga ½ hr, forestry track – Las Mimbreras ¾ hr, Las Mimbreras – Montaña Quemada 20 min, Montaña Quemada – Rejo road 25 min; total time 2¼ hrs.

Ascent: 350 m.

Grade: Easy circuit route, however expect short stretches of steep ascents and descents – consequently sure-footedness is required. Note: after heavy rainfall the passage through the tunnel should not be attempted. Bring along a powerful torch!

Refreshment: Bar/restaurant in El Cedro.

Alternative: Walkers preferring to skip the stretch through the water tunnel can begin the route at the turn-off in the road to El Cedro or in El Cedro itself.

Combination possible with Walks 39 and 43.

The forest belt encircling El Cedro presents wonderful walking opportunities – especially on hot days, pleasant rambles can be enjoyed – but these can also be extended to longer excursions. The circuit route described here is especially pretty and rich in variety, however it requires a little taste for adventure as well as an electric torch!

Starting point for the walk is the lower **hairpin bend** on the country road between the Hermigua Valley and the Cruce de la Zarcita. In the bend in the road with drystone walls and steps, a trail forks off in a northerly direction (sign). This follows parallel to power pylons and leads straight on in 2 min to

148

the entrance of a water tunnel about 500 m in length. If too much water is running through the tunnel, you must use the *camino* instead – our return route later on: this forks off to the left about 50 m after leaving the road (sign »Caserío del Cedro por el monte«). The tunnel itself brings us directly to **El Cedro**, 850 m (in the pitch-dark tunnel watch out for projecting rocks on the ceiling and for puddles!). 10 min later return into daylight (the Casa Prudencio is located immediately to the right and above).

From the tunnel exit, cross over the stream then follow the road that ascends in 5 min along the other side of the valley to the traditional **bar/restaurant »La Vista**«. Here continue climbing on the steep road to the left. After not quite another 5 min this forks at the same height as the Casa rural El Refugio – here continue the steep climb straight on along the *camino*, leaving the last houses of El Cedro behind. A few minutes later the *camino* bears right to enter the laurel forest. After a good 10 min the trail levels off. 5 min later this merges into a forestry road; ascend along this to the left. This merges already a few minutes later into another intersecting forestry road (Pista forestal a Los Aceviños y Meríga); turn left again here. Three quarter hours later, the forestry road crosses over the Cedro Stream (**Las Mimbreras**, 930 m; an excursion left to Ermita N.S. de Lourdes is worthwhile, →Walk 43).

Remain on the forestry road leading in a straight line towards the Carretera dorsal; 20 min later the road merges into a cobblestone road ascending from El Cedro. After another few minutes reach a sharp right-hand bend with low walls at the foothills of the **Montaña Quemada**, where a number of paths fork off to the left. Take the descending path forking slightly to the right (sign »El Rejo«), that forks again at the same time (do not take the narrow path forking left). This descends quite steeply, sometimes over steps, into the Rejo Valley and counts as one of the most interesting tropical forest trails on the island: garlands of ivy creepers hang from the trees and ferns up to two metres high hang over the trail. 15 min later meet up with a covered water channel and follow this to the left for a short way until the trail continues to the right, immediately after, reaching the tunnel trail that leads to the right to return to the **hairpin bend** on the Rejo road.

43 Through the Bosque del Cedro to Hermigua

Spectacular descent through the laurel forest and along the Cedro Stream – the island's cavalcade tour!

(Pajarito – Garajonay –) Alto del Contadero – Las Mimbreras – Ermita N.S. de Lourdes – El Cedro – Salto de Agua – Monteforte – El Convento

Starting point: Car park Alto del Contadero, 1350 m, on the Carretera del Centro, 1.2 km north of the road junction Pajarito (here, bus stop for line 1).

Destination: *Plaza* of El Convento, 250 m (bus stop for lines 3 and 5), one of Hermigua's highest districts.

Walking time: Alto del Contadero – Las Mimbreras 1¼ hrs, Las Mimbreras – El Cedro not quite 1 hr, El Cedro – Monteforte 1¼ hrs, Monteforte – El Convento 20 min; total time 3¾ hrs.

Descent: 1100 m.

Grade: Pleasant, easy descent to El Cedro. Afterwards, a very steep descent into the Hermigua Valley (tricky going when wet; sure-footedness required!).

Refreshment: Bar/restaurants in El Cedro

and in Hermigua.

Alternatives: From Pajarito to Alto del Contadero (½ hr): from the junction, follow the forestry road towards Garajonay (sign). 50 m on, a trail forks to the right ascending in ¼ hr to the Garajonay ridge to meet an intersecting trail (to the left along the ridge, a possible ascent to the summit of Garajonay, 10 min). To the right along the ridge, pass a *mirador*, then a good 5 min later turn right on a forestry road leading to the car park Alto del Contadero in another good 5 min.
– You can also begin the walk in Chipude (→Walk 14) or in El Cercado (→Alternative Walk 44).

Combination possible with Walks 39, 42 and 44.

The descent from the foot of Garajonay to Hermigua is the cavalcade tour of the island: this spectacular trail pulls out almost all the stops imaginable on La Gomera. As a prelude, savour the tranquillity of the magical Bosque del Cedro, seen here from its most dazzling aspect: long, beard-like strands of lichen hang down from the moss-covered trees and giant ferns liven the undergrowth. Further below, our trail is joined by the Cedro Stream, flowing with water year-round. Only shortly before reaching the hamlet of El Cedro do we leave the tropical laurel forest behind to reach a valley shelf offering an overwhelming view towards Hermigua and to the majestic Teide; to the right, the highest waterfall on the island crashes into the valley. Through pleasant cultivated terraces and at last passing the twin crags »Los Gemelos«, finally reach El Convento.

At the car park **Alto del Contadero** take the trail forking in an easterly direction (sign »El Cedro«). Climb steadily down through a shady heather tree and laurel forest along a trail that is often stepped. After ½ hr pass a small overlook with benches (terrific view of Teide and Roque de Agando). The trail continues descending along a mountain ridge. A good quarter hour later pass another overlook directly above the merry, murmuring Cedro Stream. Now it is only another 5 min to **Campamento Antiguo**, about 1060 m, where the trail forks. Take the right fork (sign »Arroyo de El Cedro«; you could actually continue to the left) then climb down to the stream and cross over this by bearing left. Now a delightful stretch follows along the bank of the Cedro Stream. A few minutes later cross over a plank to return to the left bank. Here meet up with a broad forestry trail that descends to the right to reach an intersecting forestry road (**Las Mimbreras**, 930 m; the for-

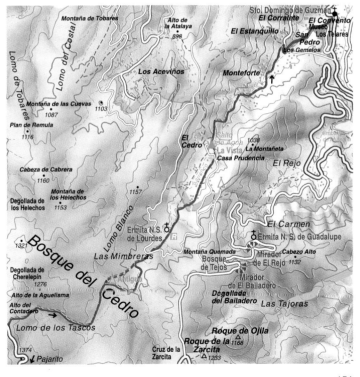

estry road leads left towards Los Aceviños, right towards the Rejo road, →Walk 42). We follow the forestry road to the right, crossing the stream and 50 m on, turn left again onto the walking trail to El Cedro (sign). This crosses the stream twice again to then reach the **Ermita de Nuestra Señora de Lourdes**, 900 m, in 10 min. The chapel, offering a number of benches and tables for a picnic, is a popular excursion destination for »Gomeros«. Passing to the right of the chapel, the descending trail continues. This leads for some minutes more along the Cedro Stream then begins to diverge away while lightly ascending to the right (always follow the main trail!) and enters a long, drawn-out clearing where the trail forks. Remain to the right on the main trail and soon pass the first houses of the hamlet **El Cedro**, 850 m. Not quite 10 min later meet up with a road that we continue along straight on. Not quite another 5 min later the road merges into a cement-paved street, leading directly past the Casa Prudencio (former bar/restaurant; to the left and below, the water tunnel that leads into the Rejo Valley →Walk 42).

Shortly after the Casa Prudencio a cobblestone trail continues, passing a property to the left. This crosses the Cedro Stream and follows the left bank, then passes the campground »La Vista« (a first-rate opportunity for refreshments in the bar/restaurant), and in a few minutes reaches a high tension

The bar/restaurant »La Vista« in El Cedro is an inviting place for a break.

View over El Cedro to the thickly-wooded heights of the central mountains.

pylon at the lower end of the mountain valley of El Cedro. Here, enjoy a view of Hermigua for the first time, with the twin crags reigning majestically over the valley. The sometimes somewhat exposed and often very steep cobblestone trail winds downward in tight bends and over uncountable steps – to the right in the cliff face, we can pick out the imposing waterfall (**Salto de Agua**, unfortunately often lacking in water). After a good half hour the most difficult stretch is behind us and we reach the floor of the Barranco de Monteforte (to the right – a pretty cascade), here continue climbing down into the valley. The cobblestone trail leads at first along the left bank then after the large dam wall changes over to the right bank. After a steep shelf, change back again to the left bank but cross back over again soon after. Over another steep shelf, climb down to a water reservoir where the *camino* returns once and for all to the left side of the valley. Always parallel to the water conduit and passing between cultivated terraces, the trail continues pleasantly on to reach Hermigua's district of **Monteforte**, 350 m, and an asphalt street. To the right along this, pass the bar »Medina Los Roques«, then later pass below the twin crags »Los Gemelos« to reach the district of **San Pedro**, 300 m. In a sharp right-hand bend, fork away from the street and continue straight on descending the broad stepped trail to finally reach our destination – the *plaza* of **El Convento** on the Carretera del Norte. Above us, on the main road, the museum Los Telares.

44 Garajonay, 1487 m

Pleasant walk along Gomera's »roof«

Laguna Grande – Alto del Contadero – Garajonay (– Pinar de Argumame – Los Manantiales – Chipude – El Cercado) – Laguna Grande

Starting point: Picnic place Laguna Grande, 1250 m, on the Carretera del Centro next to the turn-off on the road leading to Las Rosas (no bus service!). – Walkers dependent on bus service best begin the walk at the road junction at Pajarito, or the junction at Las Paredes (both bus stops for line 1), in Chipude or in El Cercado (both bus stops for lines 1, 6 and 7; →Alternatives).

Walking time: Laguna Grande – Alto del Contadero a good ¾ hr, Alto del Contadero – Garajonay 25 min, return 1–1½ hrs; total time 2¼–2¾ hrs.

Ascent: 300 m.

Grade: Mostly easy, pleasant walk via forest trails, but somewhat confusing due to numerous forks.

Refreshment: Bar/restaurant »Laguna Grande« at the starting point (closed Mondays).

Alternative: Circuit walk via Chipude and El Cercado: from Garajonay using Walk 14 to Chipude (a good 1¼ hrs, bus stop for lines 1, 6, 7). Across from the church square and to the right of the bar »La Candelaria« descend along a small cobblestone street to the main road; turn right to reach the village limits (a total of 10 min). Here, a broad cobblestone trail forks away to the left, crosses through the valley floor, then over the main road ascends to a height and on the other side, descends to El Cercado, to once again meet the main road (½ hr from Chipude).

Turn right to follow this until reaching a sharp left-hand bend (bus stop shelter). Here right onto the cobblestone road; ascend for 10 m then left climbing the cement stepped trail to reach the chapel (lovely view of the village), then turn right onto the broad trail. Soon after, at the fork, turn left passing a transformer tower, then climbing down to the broad track (this begins 100 m below at the main road). Ascend to the right along this then a few minutes later at the fork continue straight on (left), again at the next fork continue straight on (right). Soon after, the road becomes a broad *camino* and meets a broad forestry road a few minutes later. This descends to the left straight into the Barranco del Agua to cross this directly below a dam wall. Immediately after take a sharp right ascending into the valley on the forestry track that gradually leaves the vineyards behind and after a total of 40 min (from El Cercado) enter a lovely forest of pine and deciduous trees. Here at the beginning of the national park (sign), a *camino* branches off to the left to Laguna Grande (sign). This leads pleasantly through the laurisilva forest then later through an idyllic valley gap to then ascend bearing right to the bar/restaurant »Laguna Grande« (1 hr from El Cercado; circuit walk total time a good 4 hrs).

Combination possible with Walks 8, 14 and 43.

Starting point for the walk is the rest area and playground »Laguna Grande«.

When visibility is good, the route to Garajonay belongs to one of the most rewarding walks: from the overlook plateau on Gomera's highest peak enjoy an astounding view sweeping over wide expanses of the island and of the neighbouring islands of Tenerife, La Palma and El Hierro – if the sky is

very clear, even to faraway Gran Canaria. Plan and execute the walk at just the right time and not when visibility is poor.

The **Laguna Grande** picnic place is situated not far away from the mountain road and can be reached by two separate access roads that both end at the playground (car park). This is a popular excursion destination for »Gomeros«, not at least due to the excellent restaurant here (traditional food). Pass the playground to reach a baking oven about 2 metres high and made of stone at the edge of the forest. From here, a broad trail with railings leads into the laurel forest (a lovely little circuit route), which we soon leave again after a few metres by bearing left on a trail forking off. 5 min later, the path follows along the mountain road to only leave it again another good 5 min later by forking right onto the *camino forestal Chipude*. About 10 min later, a forestry road forks right towards El Cercado (our return route later on), here continue straight on along the lovely forest trail. At the next fork (not quite 5 min) turn left and, often enjoying some sunshine, ascend pleasantly (always continue straight on; do not fork to the right). After a quarter hour the forestry road merges again with the mountain road where we can take a fork again on the right side. This leads a bit away from the road and after a good 5 min merges into a forestry road that we take to the right (left on the mountain road – the car park **Alto del Contadero**, 1350 m). The for-

The ridge trail to the summit of Garajonay.

The »top« of Gomera – in clear weather, walkers swarm on the Garajonay to admire the fantastic views of Gomera and to the neighbouring islands.

estry road ascends easily and after about 20 min (always bear left at forks) reaches the overlook platform on the peak. The ridge trail that forks left in 5 min is even prettier: this ascends steadily along the ridge, leads later over a drawn-out plateau then dips down to a small saddle (10 min, trail crossing); from here continue the ascent straight on to the crest of **Garajonay** (5 min).

Walkers preferring not to return along the approach route to Laguna Grande (1 hr), can either take the circuit route via Chipude (→Alternative) or choose the following descent: on the other side of the peak platform climb down to a forestry road (house; at the same time turn right at the fork). Not quite 10 min later bear left at the fork (chain barrier), then 2 min later bear right descending steeply (sign »Laguna Grande«). 5 min after, straight on (not left), and after another 10 min ignore the trails forking right to the Pinar de Arguamé 50 m on, at the chain barrier, fork right onto the forestry road towards Laguna Grande (sign). This forks 5 min later on a dome – here descend pleasantly to the right. After a good quarter hour a forestry road merges sharply from the right (our approach route), and not quite 5 min later take a sharp left onto a forestry road towards Laguna Grande (sign), to leave this again a quarter hour later at the national park sign by bearing right onto a *camino*. This ascends mostly easily back to **Laguna Grande** (¼ hr; not quite 1½ hrs from Garajonay).

Index